THE LILAC AND THE ROSE

BY THE SAME AUTHOR

As Susan Buchan

The Sword of State

Lady Louisa Stuart

Funeral March of a Marionette

Children's Books

The Freedom of the Garden

Arabella Takes Charge

Plays

The Vision at the Inn

The Wife of Flanders

Christmas Time

Fortune

As Susan Tweedsmuir

Canada. (Britain in Pictures Series)

The Silver Ball. A novel

The Clearing House. A John Buchan Anthology

Life's Adventure. Extracts from works of J.B.

John Buchan: by His Wife and Friends.

The Rainbow through the Rain. A novel

Children's Books

Mice on Horseback

The Cat's Grandmother

The Author

THE LILAC AND THE ROSE

by

SUSAN TWEEDSMUIR

"Je n'oublierai jamais les lilas ni les roses. . . ."

GERALD DUCKWORTH & CO. LTD.
3 HENRIETTA STREET, LONDON, W.C.2

First published October 1952
Reprinted January 1953

Printed in Great Britain by
The Camelot Press Ltd., London and Southampton

TO
VIOLET MARKHAM
with love and admiration

CONTENTS

7

ILLUSTRATIONS

PREFACE

A YEAR or two ago I was walking along a street in Kensington with a young and charming companion. A thin veil of yellow mist was descending on London, and she remarked that this, she supposed, was a London fog. This led me to tell her about the fogs in my youth which shut down on London like a curtain, black and muffling. As we talked we found ourselves outside the Victoria and Albert Museum. We went inside and, after wandering about for a little while, found ourselves in a room where there were lines of glass cases, containing dolls, dressed in the costumes of different centuries.

We came to a case where there was a doll clothed in a long and elegant gown, surmounted by a very large hat. The ticket on the case bore the name of Madame Kate Reilly. This name came back to me from the past, and I recalled that Madame Kate Reilly had made my wedding gown of stiff white satin.

Kate Reilly's name has long passed into oblivion, and I have only some pieces of yellowing satin to remind me of the dress she once made for me. I thought to myself that things had come to a pretty pass when models of clothes that I had worn, or clothes like them, had become museum pieces. But it set me thinking that perhaps it was worth while to write down some of the memories which cluster round the graceful dresses of the past.

I have begun this book with family portraits, and have gone on to some reflections about my youth, or rather parts of it. I have written about various books which we read, of two winters spent in Egypt, then of balls in London and the country, and of the writers and artists I knew. I have also tried to describe country house life seen through the eyes of a young girl.

Next comes the Portrait of a House. My grandfather, Robert, 1st Lord Ebury, lived at Moor Park near Rickmansworth in Hertfordshire, and my earlier childhood was spent in this beautiful and much loved place. In the 1920s, when Moor Park was sold, my mother and I each wrote an essay describing our recollections of the house and its inmates. To these I have added a short contribution by my sister, Margaret Peyton-Jones, which shows Moor Park as seen through the eyes of a very small child. The three of us describe the same house and the same people from different points of view. I hope that this will present a good composite picture of a life that was old-fashioned (even when we knew it) and now seems archaic and outmoded in the extreme.

PART I

Family Portraits

THE GROSVENOR FAMILY

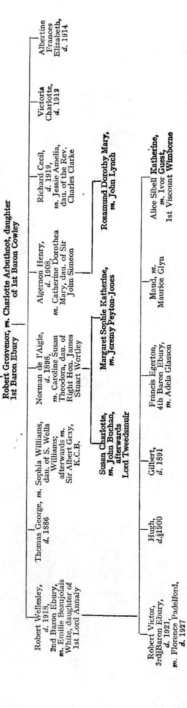

I

MY FATHER

M Y father. These two words wake in my mind so many
pleasant and happy thoughts. I see a very tall man with
dark brown eyes, whose sensitive hands always practised imaginary
finger exercises upon the arm of any chair on which he happened
to be sitting, one long leg crossed over the other. He was the
fifth of a family of five brothers and two sisters. There is a legend
that his mother showed herself averse to having so many children,
and that she was reproved by her uncle, the Duke of Wellington,
who remarked severely: "Do your duty, Charlotte, do your
duty!"—and she did.

My father had travelled as a child on the Continent in the
caravan fashion of the Victorian era. He went to Eton, and when
he grew up, joined the Grenadier Guards. He became for a time
a young man of extreme fashion who lost money racing, then
renounced the turf for ever. He left the Guards and entered the
House of Commons as Liberal Member for the family seat of
Chester, and sat for five years; then went into business as Manager
of the Sun Life Insurance; waited two years to marry my mother,
Caroline Stuart Wortley, and settled down happily with her in a
house in Green Street, with shadowy plane trees in the garden.
The house has been pulled down, the plane trees have vanished,
and there are few vestiges of green in Green Street now.

My father, who had been brought up in the strictest sect of
Whiggism, became a Liberal, or Radical, as in those days they
called his mild form of academic socialism. It is difficult now,
when we see men who profess violent opinions and are (in
Belloc's words) "accepted everywhere," to conceive that my
father was regarded as a traitor to his class by his high Tory and
Whig relations. They could not help liking him very much when
they met him, and indeed his conversation must have made a
pleasant interlude in their lives. The grandeur of their world,

with its pompous parties, endless meals and tedious weeks spent in pheasant shooting, bored him to death. He frequented the society of William Morris, Burne Jones, Edmund Gurney and William de Morgan, in whose company he breathed a freer air. He liked the easy exchange of ideas; his tenderness of heart made him extremely sensitive to human suffering and injustice, and he saw in William Morris's socialism something which promised a new dawn on a dark horizon.

Charles Booth was another of my father's friends. His book, *Life and Labour of the People*, is still a standard book often referred to by sociologists. My father helped him with his survey of the conditions of the poor in London, and valued his company as a charming talker and delightful companion.

My father was also an agnostic. This was a sore point with his family, who were devoted to church-going and to the discussion of church matters. They were all, except his mother, a little blind to the fact that he practised the Christian virtues of charity and loving kindness to an extent to which they rarely attained.

The modest and rather wistful agnosticism of that time was very different from the street-corner atheism which is fashionable to-day. It had a good deal of "reverence and godly fear," and it was essentially humble-minded. Indeed, in many ways it was more truly religious than a facile evangelicalism or an attitudinising ritualism. Men like my father and Leslie Stephen had all the major Christian virtues, the chief of which was humility.

My father had a marked talent for living, and the company of his friends delighted him. He dwelt with pleasure on their good points and was more sorry than pleased when their feet proved to be partly made of clay. He gravitated easily and naturally towards those people who were rich in interest but not in worldly goods, his greatest friend being Ben Green, the old keeper at Moor Park, with whom he had fished in the Colne and shot rabbits in the Park when he was a boy. He remained all his life a very keen fisherman. One of my happiest childish recollections is of staying at Naworth in Cumberland and sitting by the hour together on the banks of the Eden reading Andrew Lang's fairy tales. I looked up occasionally at my father's tall figure in ancient tweeds

My Father and
Myself

Norman de L'Aigle
Grosvenor

Grosvenor House in 1927

Reproduced from the drawing by Hanslip Fletcher by courtesy of the 'Sunday Times'

with a cap (ornamented by salmon flies) pulled down over his forehead. He fished with the steady carefulness of the born angler, covering every yard of water. (He was also very good at tennis and golf, an aptitude not transmitted to his daughters, whose mixed boredom and incompetence when forced to join in any kind of game were a by-word in the family.) He loved old clothes, and met with steady resistance every attempt on the part of my mother to impound worn-out suits, to give them to jumble sales.

My father enjoyed the discussion of all manner of problems, and was an easy and delightful talker, and the best of listeners. Discussion, like the whole of life in those days, was a leisurely affair, for the world did not move with such rapid and dangerous velocity as in the nineteen-fifties, and the opinions of intelligent men and women outside the political arena counted far more than they do now. He was a passionate lover of music, but had begun to study a little late in life for the full mastery of an art. On his return from his office he would go straight to his piano and work at technique like a girl at a musical academy. Few professional musicians have attended more strictly to their musical education, playing those endless scales and finger exercises which are woven into all my bedtime memories, and were the prelude to those dreamless nights which depart with childhood. He also studied harmony and counterpoint by the hour together.

Among those who came to our house (30 Upper Grosvenor Street, which has vanished to give place to the block of luxury flats known as Grosvenor House) was Dr. (later Sir) Walford Davies, who was to do so much for English and Welsh music. Walford Davies helped my father to start an organisation in the poorer quarters of London. It was named The People's Concert Society, and was the parent of many popular musical movements in England. It came to an end some years ago, the need for it having ceased. But in the days before gramophones, wireless, and concerts with cheap seats were available to everybody, it did a great deal to dispel the fiction that the English are a completely unmusical race. The music played at these concerts was severely classical, and any attempt to insert items of popular music in The People's Concert Society's programmes met with disfavour on the part of its patrons, who, while paying a few pence for their seats, demanded the best available music for their money. It was a valuable experiment in adult education because it established the fact beyond doubt that the poorest class of citizens are often those who have the most distinguished musical taste. This is a commonplace to-day, but was a completely new idea to most people when my father conceived his idea of a popular musical society.

My father much disliked posing, flashy, artificial people, and he could be unbendingly severe in their company. I remember once, when a fashionable actress had been invited to lunch, over-hearing my mother say afterwards, "I saw by the set of Norman's shoulders how much he disliked her." But this sort of incident happened rarely. My father is remembered by those who knew him as bringing a kind of mellowness into any company, the pleasure which comes to one in a garden on a sunny afternoon. He always gave me a sense of security when I was with him, and I rushed to him during thunderstorms, mental and physical, and felt completely safe and sheltered. Although I was never anything of a musician I loved to hear him play, and would listen to his own compositions, his symphonies, and exquisite settings of *A Child's Garden of Verses*, by the hour together. I feel sure that these little-known melodies of his will some day sound again.

When he died, the darkened house and hushed voices of the family and our friends left a deep scar on my mind. He died at the age of fifty-three after a long and painful illness. He remained serene, courageous, and calm to the end. He lay in a room filled with flowers and his friend Susan Lushington played the violin to him. His last words were: "Beauty is one of the last toys we play with."

2

MY MOTHER

MY father died in middle age and my mother lived to be over eighty. She died in 1940 during the Battle of Britain. We dimly realised, when we were children, that our parents' life together was ideally happy. They had fallen in love with each other in youth and had remained so until death parted them.

My parents were both members of large Victorian families. They both of them had that power to give and take, and of respecting other people's points of view, which was one of the advantages of family life in the grand manner. They were united in their love of music and painting. My mother was not musical, but her brother Charles and her sister Margaret were both admirable musicians, and she could enjoy concerts and talk intelligently about music. She played the piano a little herself, though she did not give much time to it.

My father was a discriminating lover of pictures, and he helped and encouraged my mother with her painting, at which she worked very seriously indeed. She had a pronounced artistic bent, and her miniatures of her friends, her watercolours and her embroidery are admirable by any standards.

Nowadays when women are able to sell their work on equal terms with men, she could have made a living with her portraits. As it was, only relations and friends gave her commissions for miniatures. This was for some reason considered right. I do not quite know why, but I imagine her prices were of a ladylike sparseness. What she received cannot have helped the family budget very much.

My father did not care much for entertaining with large dinner parties, but they had many intimate evenings with their friends, when music and conversation alternated in a pleasant way. My mother entertained her friends a great deal at five o'clock, and in those days men as well as women went out to tea. I can see in retrospect my mother's drawing-room with the big shaded lamps on the tables, and the pools of shadow beyond them. She sat behind a tea table, on which were ranged many plain brown cups and saucers. It is hard to see why she chose them in those days when really beautiful china was an heirloom in most families, and new and prettily painted cups were easy to obtain. Some people thought the brown china odd and unconventional. To our eyes it would look only too like utility stuff, but "Caroline Grosvenor's brown cups" became a sort of institution amongst her friends and relations; something to be affectionately smiled at as the fad of a beloved friend.

My mother got on well with servants, who stayed for decades. Our food was good and simple, and our house was clean though shabby in parts, but there were some good pieces of furniture which gave dignity to any room they were in. She never bothered about keeping everything in the house up to date; she had so many things to do which interested her more.

She was tall, straight-backed, and fair-haired. People thought her handsome rather than pretty. She had been made to wear glasses by an oculist at the age of twenty-three to correct an astigmatism. She could look sternly at people through them, and was sometimes thought alarming on that account. But she was shy, with a shyness that stemmed from a Victorian upbringing, when the elders in a family pointed out incisively any mistake or clumsiness committed by a younger member of the family.

My mother had very definite artistic standards and would have scorned to let it be supposed that she ever could countenance for a moment any kind of second-rate or spurious work; but she was able to give discriminating admiration to much of the work of modern artists which many of her contemporaries regarded with horrified amazement.

After my father died, my mother wished to erect a monument to him in the churchyard at Northwood in Middlesex. She decided to design a headstone for his grave, and to work on a plaster cast of it. This proved to be the labour of years. She had done clay modelling in her youth, and she settled down, after her design was finished, to wrestle with all the problems of large-scale modelling in intractable material. She was helped by an elderly German sculptor, who gave advice when the clay was too wet or too dry, and there were days when our whole horizon seemed to be bounded by these two factors. At last the head-stone·was finished and was sent to be cast in bronze. It stands to-day as a memorial of a wife to her husband, and is, I believe, now mentioned in a guide-book as a monument not to be missed.

My mother never really had good health and she took a very deep interest in illness. She would discuss medical subjects with her friends and her sisters with the keenest possible zest. "Symptoms" were a favourite topic, and as everyone in her circle had their own pet physician an awkwardness could arise at a cosy tea-party if anyone ventured to throw doubts on the skill of a family doctor. A silence could also fall if anyone admitted that they had unfaithfully consulted a new and untried specialist.

Any remarks such as "Well, your Dr. Blank didn't do so-and-so much good" could raise a tea-cup storm which would not subside for a time, and might leave a drop of bitterness in the cup ever afterwards.

My mother moved at a slow *tempo* as she grew older, and she greatly disliked the pace at which people moved in the 1920s and 1930s. Snap decisions and rapid readjustments were not for her; she constantly said "I must think this over" or "Let me collect my wits" when asked to take the most trivial decisions. If further pressed, she would ask for more time to brood over the matter which, by that time, had reached elephantine proportions.

When my mother left 30 Upper Grosvenor Street she went to a small house on the opposite side nearer to Grosvenor Square. She did not admire the cliff-like block of flats which had blotted out so many smaller and more charming buildings, but she lived happily, daily entertaining some friend or other, and regarding her grandchildren, who came in and out, with a far more indulgent eye than she had accorded to her own children.

In 1939, at the outbreak of war, she was persuaded to move down to Elsfield, where she spent the last months of her life. She thought the country pretty dreary, but as her health declined I think she was glad to be there.

After my mother died I had many letters from people to whom she had been kind and generous. Some people who wrote said they felt that a landmark had gone, and that they had not only lost a good friend, but someone who symbolised to them the integrity and stateliness of an older world.

3

AUNT LILY

I HAVE written of my father and mother and shall now try to describe Magdalen Wellesley—Lily, or Aunt Lily as we called her, our great-aunt.

She was the daughter of Henry Robinson Montagu, Lord Rokeby. This takes us into a remote past, as he was born in 1798, was present at Quatre Bras and Waterloo, and commanded a division in the Crimea.

His daughter, Magdalen Montagu, married in 1856 Gerald Wellesley, the Dean of Windsor, my grandmother Charlotte Ebury's brother. They had one son, to whom Queen Victoria stood sponsor and who died young.

These are the bare bones of the story. My mother always told me that Aunt Lily was so supremely lovely in her youth that she was nicknamed "The Measles," as falling in love with her was the inevitable fate of all the young men who met her. She had many offers of marriage and surprised everyone by marrying the Dean of Windsor, an austere man much older than herself. I remember her in her old age, and whenever I go along Lower Berkeley Street (the very name of which has been changed) I sigh. How I wish that I could put back the hands of the clock and stand on the doorstep of No. 7, knowing with certainty that the door whose bell I had rung would be opened by a round-faced, elderly footman-butler, who would reply "Yes" to my question if Mrs. Wellesley were at home.

Moving hastily towards a door, he and I would collide, as

22

he tried to get in front and formally announce me, and I would then find myself in a warm little room full of books, photographs, and ornaments where two old ladies in black were sitting, sewing and knitting garments for the poor. I would find myself embraced and, after a confusion of greetings and a kiss planted on Aunt Cinny's cushion-like cheek (Aunt "Cinny" was Aunt Lily's sister, Elizabeth Montagu), I would settle down comfortably to talk and listen.

Aunt Lily's beauty was little impaired by age, the severe bandeaux of hair framing her face only serving to emphasise its harmonies and the charm of her expression. There was something so merry as well as so kind in the way she looked at you that you could hardly help laughing for pleasure, and when you left her, stayed with tea, cakes, a great deal of news and invariably a gift, the glow of her presence was like a tangible, comforting atmosphere accompanying you.

Human beings in their power of giving out affection seem to me to resemble fires. Some give light without heat, some a gusty, flickering flame, some go out altogether after their youth is passed. Only a few can keep up an even, steady warmth which circumstances cannot alter. Of the few who have had that power, Aunt Lily was pre-eminent, and she triumphantly stood the test of time. At the age of eighty-eight neither length of years, nor physical pain, nor sorrow, had weakened her power of loving and of giving happiness to all who came near her.

To describe a person who is dead and whom one has loved is perhaps impossible. One may pile the Pelion of adjective upon the Ossa of qualities, and leave no effect on the reader's mind but a feeling of satiety and a devout wish never to hear of the subject again. This is especially true of memoirs of women who have played no great part in public affairs, and who have added to the happiness of the few, instead of dazzling the many. If we could draw aside the curtain which hangs between us and Aunt Lily's youth and see her, wonderfully young, gay, and lovely at a London ball or at Queen Victoria's Court at Windsor, we should get a brilliant vision enchanting to the casual reader. The pen of the dullest of us would find glowing words to describe something as radiant as she must have been. A much harder task is to make intelligible the fact that this old lady was the centre of so many people's lives, and so necessary to them for their happiness and cheer.

At her death one heard none of the glib philosophy of youth or middle age in phrases like: "Well, well, he or she has had a run for their money" or "Ah, well, people can't live for ever. She has had a long time of it." To the people who loved her, her death came with the cutting force and that feeling of blank sorrow usually felt for those who die in youth too soon.

When I was a child some lingering essence of Puritanism distilled into every generation since the Great Rebellion, inclined my judgment to the conclusion that the "extra good" must show it in every line, in a rigidity of manner and behaviour, and should, in fact, wear their goodness like a spiritual strait-waistcoat. I can quite well remember a strong sensation of surprise that Aunt Lily (who dressed in the black silk which to my mind betokened age and extreme virtue) never pulled a long face, but told amusing stories, joked, laughed, and had nicknames for nearly everyone. She was entirely without conventionality in an age which worshipped that useful goddess blindly. I remember when my grandmother Lady Ebury died, and I, as a very small, trembling child, was led into her austere bedroom where she lay calm and beautiful in death, Aunt Lily held my hand tightly and talked in her ordinary voice. She saw no reason for the gruesome whisperings so terrifying to children, which are supposed to be a sign of sorrow and a tribute to the dead, and yet she had loved my grandmother with a love passing that of most sisters and mourned her deeply, never ceasing to talk of her.

When I was very small, I spent a halcyon few days with Aunt Lily at Farnham Royal, in a pleasant, red-brick, creeper-muffled house with a sort of Georgian aura about it. I received great kindness from her circle of old retainers, who had known nearly all my father's family well, and extended their interest to me. I wandered joyfully about the house, which, like all those decorated by the early Victorians, was deeply interesting to children.

Everything was a jumble, for in taste they were real democrats and believed in equality of opportunity. A sixpenny china cup bought at Bournemouth was put in equal prominence with an exquisite piece of Crown Derby or Worcester, while the tables, crowded with miscellaneous treasures, promised endless delights, as did the dark-coloured walls on which pictures, good, bad, and indifferent, faced the world shoulder to shoulder. I have a vague recollection of being naughty and elbowing a little boy into a pond by the road, but my chief remembrance is of a cow who lived in the quiet meadow beyond the garden. "That," said Aunt Lily, "I call the Beastly Cow." I was enchanted by the name and still more by the fact that the cow, regarding human beings with obvious distaste, rushed to the fence whenever I approached, mooing with rage. The fence was substantial, and I could afford to laugh at my adversary, and so played the game of running toward the field clapping my hands freely. For years afterwards I asked wistfully after the Beastly Cow, and the episode remained always a great joke between us. Aunt Lily loved jokes above all things, and stories of all kinds, especially of the grotesque misfortunes of humanity such as being sick, swallowing false teeth, etc. These, combined with her goodness and deeply spiritual outlook, made a most piquant contrast.

I spoke before of the inversion of roles of old and young, and will try to make my point clear. I have often heard young people say, "I *must* go and see my old aunt so-and-so and cheer her up." Where Aunt Lily was concerned these words would have died on their lips. You didn't cheer Aunt Lily; she cheered you. You never knew as many good stories as she did. The latest gossip was far more at her command than at yours. Dull and *blasé* young people were apt to leave Aunt Lily's company much lighter in heart, shaken out of their apathy, and with a feeling of envy that, after a life of many years, filled with much experience, many sorrows and a lion's share of physical suffering, she could still find so much good in the world, and think it such a supremely amusing place.

In her judgments of people she was remarkably acute. She never judged anyone unheard, and always tried to understand their temptations. When she did judge severely, she could be severe indeed; but this seldom happened.

Her most important piece of work, carried on unobtrusively all her life, was a home for girls at Clewer. It was for those who had taken that step in life which is a moral glissade into depths from which ascent is difficult. Aunt Lily's love must have helped many of them to hold up their heads again, and get back to the fairway of life. Her charity altogether was unending and, like her moral judgments, understanding and forgiving.

The most salient feature of her character was a passion for giving. A French lady of the eighteenth century, surprised alone on a Sunday evening by a worldly acquaintance, was seen to be putting small sums of money into bags. She explained this on the grounds that sometimes she was *d'humeur donnante*. Aunt Lily was never in any other humour. I have never been to see her without receiving some present or other. She always had an apparently inexhaustible supply somewhere near. Just as one rose to say goodbye, she would put her hand into a drawer and bring out something. She also liked getting presents, especially anything quaint or funny, and never gave you that overwhelmed feeling which those who like giving, but not receiving, are apt to do. She also gave her sympathy, her love, her time, all day long to everyone who needed them. Giving, to her, was as easy as breathing, and as absolute a necessity.

Aunt Lily and Aunt Cinny revelled in the horrible and frightening, as well as in the grotesque, and could cap each other's tales of illness and accidents, which would have been unnerving had they not been told with such cosy cheerfulness and humour.

I remember (the only time, happily, that I can recall such a thing) Aunt Lily being vexed with me. When sitting by her bedside in London during 1915, she told me a specially terrifying prophecy of how, when the Zeppelins came, as must happen shortly, all the German waiters in London would swarm on to the roofs of houses, armed with machine guns, and shoot us all down. "Well, that's not likely to come true, anyway," was my thoughtless comment, which the next moment I wished unsaid, as I saw that she really believed it and was hurt by my scepticism.

Aunt Cinny died in 1917, and the lack of her kind and gentle presence was a great loss to all who knew her. Aunt Lily missed her, I feel sure, every moment of the day. She had to leave the house at Farnham Royal, where she had lived for so long, and settle in a small house nearby. She was content with it, and delighted to show off its humdrum modern conveniences—bathrooms, lights, etc.—to all who came. Only the very selfish amongst us could have wished her to live on. It was in September, 1919, that the message came to her, as to Bunyan's Pilgrim, that "her Master was not willing that she should be so far from Him any longer."

4

AUNT MAMIE

MY mother's eldest sister, whom her nieces called Aunt Mamie, was *née* Mary Stuart Wortley. She was the eldest of a family of nine brothers and sisters, and my mother, who was ten years her junior, regarded her as belonging to their mother's generation.

Aunt Mamie's life span was a long one. She was born in 1848 and remembered all her life being carried, as a very small child, to her nursery window overlooking the Mall. She saw a lumbering carriage on which flickering lights showed broad gleams of scarlet and gold, and she heard a trampling of horses and jingling of bits and bridles. As the sounds died away she was told always to remember that she had seen the Duke of Wellington's funeral.[1] When telling this story, she added that what she saw must have been the passing of the coffin on its way from Stratfieldsaye to Chelsea Hospital where the Duke lay in state before the final ceremonies. His funeral took place in broad daylight, watched by a great concourse of people. Aunt Mamie lived to be over ninety and died during World War II to the sound of bombers going over her house.

[1] The Duke of Wellington's funeral took place on November 18th, 1852.

She grew up in London and spent her girlhood in a small house in St. James's Place. It was packed tight with a large family, her father, crippled by a stroke, and her mother gallantly coping with increasingly straitened means. She ardently wished to study painting, and she put all the force of an exceptionally strong will into becoming an artist. She decided to have a training at the Slade School in Gower Street. Her parents always bent to her will, and they agreed to this.

It is almost impossible to realise in these days how difficult it was for Aunt Mamie to do the apparently simple journey from St. James's Place to Gower Street. When she was young, no girl of *quality* (the italics are hers) could be seen alone in the street without scandal. She had to leave home too early for the schoolroom party and their governess to be free to go with her. Her mother's maid was busy with the much more congenial task of running up the seams of cheap stuff for ball dresses for the young ladies, and the daily ride in a four-wheeler (hansoms were barred as being too exposed to the public gaze) was much too expensive to be contemplated.

However, by sheer force of character and insistence she managed to get an escort through the danger zone of Bond Street and Regent Street, where friends and acquaintances might be met. Then, alone, she embarked on a quick rush through the remaining streets till she reached the Slade, and she told me amusingly of her terror lest any friends, returning in a luggage-laden four-wheeler from King's Cross or Euston, should catch a glimpse of her.

After all these dangers were past, she stood at her easel all day, walked to within a shilling fare for a cab in the evening, and came home to amuse her invalid father.

I should like to be able to record that she was a great artist. If hard work and unflagging will power could have made her so, she would have been one; but her work, though faithful and accurate, was never more than mediocre.

Mary Stuart-Wortley married at the age of thirty-two (rather an advanced age for those days) Ralph Lord Wentworth, afterwards Earl of Lovelace. After her marriage she went on painting and took some training as an architect. She planned the building and improvement of the cottages on her husband's estates. She also took a leading part in any movements for the revival of arts and crafts, and she constantly voiced her conviction that people should not buy antique furniture and old pictures, but patronise and support the arts of their own day. She was an ardent admirer of William Morris and of the architect Voysey, and their influence led her down strange paths. A stucco classical arcade, which ran half along the front of the house at Ockham, was done away with and replaced by one in a quasi-Dutch style of Voysey's design. Worse was to follow when some fine panelling, dating from the eighteenth century and put into the house by Ralph Lovelace's ancestor, Lord Chancellor King, was swept away. Aunt Mamie announced that it was meretricious and wanting in sincerity. She banned old furniture as *bric-à-brac*, and bought pottery from the market places of the Continent, and plain unornamented tables, sideboards and rugs from the Home Arts Society, of which she was one of the moving spirits. Her sisters did not approve of all this, but she brooked no criticism and went her own way.

Their houses were comfortable, but Ralph Lovelace had a horror of plumbing, and Aunt Mamie agreed with him in this. She deplored the spread of bathrooms, saying that there was no reason why the countryside should be drained of water in order that the middle classes might wash in comfort. The lack of plumbing in a large country house is always a surprising thing, and guests had to put up with hip baths which were filled from large pewter ewers, and other inconveniences.

During the First World War she put all the dynamic energy that she had put into her painting, into the reconstruction of the little harbour at Porlock Weir near the Lovelace property of Ashley Combe. For years this had been falling into decay. The mole at its entrance was giving way, the fishermen's houses on the sea front were threatened by the inroad of the sea, the harbour was useless. At that stage of the war (1916) the need for pit props in the mines, which were working full time to supply the Navy, was acute. In the woods round Ashley there was plenty of timber, but without a harbour in which to load the vessels this timber could not be made use of for the purpose. Aunt Mamie stirred up local opinion, formed a small joint-stock company, induced the well-to-do people of the neighbourhood, as well as many who lived further afield, to take shares in the company, and in a few months had the satisfaction of seeing shiploads of timber crossing the Bristol Channel to South Wales. Small wonder that in that corner of Somerset her name was held in high reverence.

Aunt Mamie was in some ways a formidable aunt to her various nieces. She had none of the modern admiration for youth as youth, in fact she thought rather poorly of the young. I can see her now looking at me very straight, as she voiced some sharp criticism of my behaviour.

She was of middle height and not slim. She disliked corsets, thinking them unhygienic, so that her figure was not her strong point. She looked her best in the evening when she wore a flowing black silk or satin dress which enhanced her natural dignity. She wore long looped gold chains from which dangled a massive diamond heart. She had a straight profile and pretty slightly untidy hair drawn back from a low broad forehead.

My mother told us that Aunt Mamie's life was not an easy one and hinted that people who were living difficult lives often said sharp things to their relations. As we grew older we became fonder and fonder of Aunt Mamie and more at ease with her. No one who had any glimmerings of intelligence could fail to be interested in talking to her about her architectural work (or indeed on any other subject), and she showed us an endless generosity and kindness.

I think that the circumstances of her life had made her go on living in the climate of her youth. This was not in a way surprising as she moved in an orbit between Ockham Park, Ashley Combe, and Wentworth House, varied by trips to small and remote inns in the Alps, as her husband was a noted mountaineer. It is difficult for anyone in these days to know just how secluded life in country houses could be. It was a well-ordered life with design and plan in it, and in Aunt Mamie's case a very hard-working one. The studio in which she worked with large tables covered with architects' plans bore witness to this, and she was always accessible to give help and advice to all the tenants on the two estates—and I know that not only personal but financial help was ungrudgingly given.

My uncle and aunt's friends were not very numerous but mostly had intellectual distinction, and to all relations, even to the most remote cousins, Aunt Mamie's kindness never flagged or faltered. But somehow none of this brought her into any kind of main stream of life, and Aunt Mamie developed in youth and middle age a fierce suspicion of anything new just because it was new.

She did have a bathroom and a car towards the end of her life, but spoke slightingly of them, and when the telephone was installed at Wentworth House she disliked it intensely, remarking to my mother that after you lifted the receiver to your ear all you heard "was a doll squeaking in Hindustani miles away." (There have been moments when after a prolonged struggle to get the right number I have been tempted to echo this arbitrary judgment.)

Aunt Mamie's strictures on the looks and behaviour of her nieces' contemporaries sometimes provoked a sullen sense of rebellion in us. She constantly criticised our clothes, and as we considered hers extremely dowdy this reduced us to a resentful silence. I remember a lecture she once gave me when I appeared in a green dress of which I was very proud. She told me sternly that a green dress never looked right in the country "because" (and as she delivered this judgment she waved her hand to the spreading cedars and wide lawns in the garden) "of all the greenery outside," an argument I can follow as little now as I did then.

We had very little money in those days with which to buy clothes, and therefore we had to wear the criticised garments at Ockham again and again. To do Aunt Mamie justice, she refrained from further criticism, but we felt awkward all the same.

My husband and she always liked each other. She had mellowed by the time they met and he delighted in her forthright remarks, and when she found that he was sympathetic she became gayer and more amusing when he was there. We stayed with her once or twice at Wentworth House. My bedroom overlooked the Chelsea herb garden. From the drawing-room one could see the restless river and hear the little waves slapping against the wall of the Embankment. Later our daughter Alice was married from Wentworth House, and so it became linked up with happiness for us. But it was a house which held little gaiety in spite of its beautiful position and the charm of many of its rooms. It was always a silent house; it needed cheerful and noisy children to bring it to life.

Ashley Combe, the house where the Lovelaces lived for part of every year, was set in lovely surroundings. I remember staying there one autumn when I was a girl, and walking for hours among dripping woods in a warm, wet atmosphere which always made me feel rather tired. The sea seemed almost too lazy to do more than gently lap the shingled beach below the house with tiny waves. I liked going inland, where there were smooth green valleys, and being shown the farm still inhabited by descendants of the Ridds in *Lorna Doone*. This appealed very much to my sense of romance. I also enjoyed gathering great branches of glossy green leaves with round strawberry-coloured berries.

The only aspect of life at Ashley Combe which I thoroughly disliked was Aunt Mamie's addiction to parrots. Hers were small, bright green and scarlet in colour, and made a disproportionate amount of noise for their size. She loved them dearly and they her, and they played charmingly with her gold chains and sat on her shoulder. But they did not like or approve of her guests, and they had a very trying habit of wandering about under the dining-room table at meal-times. One of them viciously bit my foot during dinner, and Aunt Mamie was very severe to me when I made a slight fuss about this. She reprobated, what she called "cowardice about parrots," and was in fact unimaginative, like many other people who forget that a much-loved dog, cat, or parrot can be a nuisance to everyone except their owner.

Mary Countess of Lovelace in Her Wedding Dress

Mrs. Gerald Wellesley (Aunt Lily)—a Victorian Bedroom

Aunt Mamie

Aunt Mamie, as I have said, was very fond of her nieces, but Helen Maclagan[1] was more like a daughter to her than any member of her family. Helen's death during World War II left her large circle of friends with a deep and abiding sense of loss. She had a fine and commanding presence. Her face was small and her nose tip-tilted. Being short-sighted, she looked at the world through round spectacles, although when she was at a party she used very long tortoiseshell lorgnettes. A warmth and glow came from her, and she had a golden quality of kindness. Helen had a quick sense of humour and when she differed from you, which she frequently did, it was at once and with emphasis; an argument with Helen was always stimulating and interesting.

She had also great practical gifts. I remember the last time that I saw her was in the early autumn of 1940 when Eric and she stayed at Elsfield for a week. I think of Helen in our orchard, enveloped in a white overall, in the depths of a plum tree, industriously picking plums in order that not one should be wasted.

When Helen's friends wanted her sympathy (which they did constantly), she would go long distances to see them by the most severely democratic forms of transport. She and Aunt Mamie were alike in some ways; in their dislike of second-rateness, and of easy solutions to problems, and both were forthright in speech and action. Helen lived in an interesting milieu, and she interpreted to Aunt Mamie the contemporary scene in thought and action better than anyone else was able to do.

Uncle Ralph—the mere writing down of his name makes him come vividly before me. He had a stocky figure and was usually dressed in slightly eccentric clothes. He had a fine head with greying hair, usually a little wild, a pointed nose, and small dark eyes. As I say, his clothes were a little strange; he wore a jacket made of Loden cloth brought from Austria, grey flannel trousers and string shoes on which he padded silently about the house and garden. When we were children we felt him to be nice but formidable—children live their lives on sufferance in other people's houses, at any moment they may transgress by trampling

[1] Née Helen Lascelles; she married Sir Eric Maclagan.

on rose beds, or by breaking windows and giggling at meals. I should imagine that Uncle Ralph would not have minded any of these misdemeanours very much, though it was not safe to take any chances about that. Aunt Mamie *did* mind when complaints were brought to her by servants or gardeners, but she regarded children as necessary nuisances who were born to do tiresome things.

More alarming to us than her scoldings was the realisation that Aunt Mamie carefully steered the conversation away from all topics which would cause her husband to fly into an angry rage. His dark eyes could look very fierce indeed, and with the strange inconsequence of a child, they always reminded me of an elephant's eyes. Someone had told me that when an elephant is angry its eyes grow red, and I watched Uncle Ralph's constantly out of the corner of my pale, childish orbs to see if this was going to happen.

Uncle Ralph had a way of vanishing to his room in a wing of the house at Ockham, where he played the violin. He was not a particularly good performer on this instrument—in fact, there was something intensely mournful about the sounds which issued from his window—but I imagine that playing on any instrument, however unsuccessfully you do it, must be an excellent outlet for anger or frustration.

As I write, my admiration increases for my mother's sister. Aunt Mamie had the highest possible ideal of wifely duty, and one part of it consisted in listening to, and being interested in, everything her husband wished to tell her. She had to hear endlessly about his grandmother, Lady Byron, and about the wickedness of Byron's publishers, of inheritances and wills, and generally about a world which aimed darts at Uncle Ralph from every direction. Aunt Mamie was by nature a very impatient woman, but the way she schooled herself to be patient showed the real strength and sweetness of her disposition. My mother and I always felt specially sorry for her because she had never been helped by a feeling of glamour about Byron. She did not care for his poetry, and his personality held for her none of the strange lure which it held for so many people in his own country, and on the con-

tinent of Europe. (As I write in 1951, this interest has by no
means spent itself.)

About Byron's private life she could have had no curiosity
left; the story had been told to her so often by Byron's grand-
son. The whole Byron saga became a sheer weariness to her,
a weariness shot with a constant alarm, that there would be
something published about Byron or his wife which would
make Uncle Ralph angry or unhappy.

Aunt Mamie read a good deal, but she was not much interested
in writers except Henry James, William De Morgan, and Hugh
Walpole, all three of whom she knew well. But on the whole
she far preferred architects and craftsmen as companions.

As we grew up we became very fond of Uncle Ralph. He
liked young people and talked to his wife's nieces about their
various interests. He and I always talked about literature, and
he would go off and look for books in his library; I remember
becoming almost walled up by piles of volumes while he lucidly
expounded passages from them.[1] He was very kind to my sister
and me as he had been very fond of our father.

When Ralph Lovelace died we all mourned him, and my
mother and aunts were specially sad because, as life had gone
on, Aunt Mamie and he had settled down to a married life of
happiness and understanding.

Aunt Mamie writes of her husband's death in her memoirs
of him:

"The late summer of 1906 was hot and oppressive. For some
reason we did not seek coolness at Ashley Combe, but lingered
on at Ockham. One sultry morning in August, the head wood-
man came to report damage by mischievous boys in Lovelace's
favourite plantation. Very wrathful, he sallied forth in the hot
sun to the scene of destruction, and came back much heated and
tired. That afternoon we had a visit from Mr. Francis Galton,[2]

[1] In writing to Uncle Ralph after the publication of *Astarte*, Henry James
says: "I can but admire and envy you the magnificence of the fund on which
you so liberally draw, I mean your fund of reading and historic saturation."

[2] Later Sir Francis Galton, anthropologist, traveller, and founder of the
science of eugenics.

most charming of talkers, kindest and most accessible of cele-
brated men. There was long and delightful conversation between
him and Lovelace on the terrace, and Mr. Galton amused himself as usual in our aviary, being especially charmed with the
love-drama between Pierrot, the green Amazon parrot, and Rosy
Talbot, the pink cockatoo, a recent gift from my sister in Australia. The last word that my husband addressed to me was some
joke about Pierrot and his ardent courtship.

"An hour later he was found on that same terrace, lying on
his face in the twilight. He had passed away without fear or pain."

PART II

Foreword to Youth

READING

I WAS a member of a family in which the grown-ups were always reading and talking about their books. In a world where there were no cinemas, radio programmes, or motor cars and where the greatest excitement was a magic-lantern lecture or a drive in a wagonette to a picnic, books were our only outlet to a wider world.

Not all parents really care for reading, but those whom I knew in my youth were aware that books should play a part in life. Children were read aloud to a great deal, and my mother and father and their friends talked about books constantly in front of us, which made us feel that reading was an exciting and adult thing to do.

We had few books compared to the children nowadays, and when we were given a book it was not something to be read and discarded, but a valued, friendly possession to which we returned constantly. We got to know whole chapters of our favourite books by heart, and we recited them to each other, always discovering new points of interest in them.

I learned to read in a book exquisitely illustrated by Walter Crane. It had pictures of cats on mats, and of boys with bats. I also had a Kate Greenaway alphabet with pictures of little girls in poke bonnets with wide sashes round their waists. I went on from this to *Reading without Tears*. There was a story in it called "Bertie's Donkey" for which I had a special affection. It described how a shawled and bonneted lady took her children for a picnic to the seaside. After a lavish tea (described in full detail), the lady thought that the sea water would be good and strengthening for the donkey's legs. The animal in question stood stock still and refused to move, so she tied a shawl round his head and led him into the water. The donkey, much bewildered, went further and further into the sea till he was completely out of his depth. Fortunately, a fisherman was rowing a small boat

nearby. He grabbed hold of the donkey's bridle and towed it
back to the shore, remarking under his breath that someone
who blindfolded a donkey and pushed it into the sea was as big
an ass as the animal in question.

In contrast to this stupid but opulent lady in *Reading without
Tears*, I loved a book called *Little Meg's Children* about a family
of orphans who were sunk in dire poverty, until they discovered
a box of golden sovereigns under a bed and lived happily ever
after. My husband in his childhood also revelled in a deeply senti-
mental story called *Froggy's Little Brother*, about a virtuous but
pallid and pathetic child; and when any member of our family
tried to pull out the stop of pathos, he always remarked devastatingly, "You remind me of Froggy's little brother."

I was captivated by tales of China, and Aunt Sophie[1] was always
there to tell us about her Chinese childhood. At Moor Park there
were many Chinese objects, and I drowned in a sea of *chinoiserie*.
I could hardly be torn away from looking at the Chinese wall-
papers, and even a willow pattern plate had to be firmly covered
by porridge or pudding before I would stop staring at it. I
gazed longingly up at the figures which stood on mantelpieces
and on the tops of cabinets well out of a child's reach. When
I read *The Cuckoo Clock* by Mrs. Molesworth I felt like a member of a secret society who has been given a password. The
child's ride on the cuckoo's back, between two rows of nodding
mandarins, confirmed my belief that those silent porcelain figures
had a secret nocturnal life of their own.

At nine years old I suddenly woke up to the excitement of
historical romance. My mother gave me *Ivanhoe* and a whole
world of knights, ladies, tournaments as well as the resistance
movement of the Saxons against the Normans swam into my
ken. *Ivanhoe* opened my eyes to the fact that history is the most
entrancing subject in the world, and I have made it my study
ever since.

I was an incurably romantic child, and while staying at Naworth
in Cumberland, which began by being a Border castle, I fell on
Andrew Lang's *Gold of Fairnilee*, which tells of the Scottish side

[1] See page 107.

of the Border and of the River Tweed. I revelled in this fascinating tale where the hero is enticed away from his home by the Fairy Queen. Years after when I married a Scotsman from the Borders, we went to visit Fairnilee, and although there was no golden treasure and no Fairy Queen, tears of excitement came into my eyes, and I felt as if I had come home.

I knew a great many English and Scottish ballads by heart and I liked even the fiercest of them, and could calmly recite

"And never a word spake Kinmont Willie
But thrust his lance through his false bodie."

Stories of "lifted" (stolen) cattle, burning farmhouses, desperate rides in the moonlight over peat bogs and through flooded rivers did not frighten me at all.

The Jungle Books were my next revelation of a different kind of romance to *Ivanhoe*. To children with any talent for acting the scenes in *The Jungle Books* are pure joy. With a group of cousins at Northiam in Sussex, where my grandmother, Mrs. Stuart Wortley, had a house, we took the parts of Akela, Bagheera, and Kaa in all moments spared from lessons or outdoor pursuits. I remember that there was not much competition for the part of Mowgli; we may have felt that beasts were more satisfactory than human beings from the histrionic point of view. I am always sorry for children who have no love of drama, and cannot delve deep into a book and get fun out of it with the crudest kind of childish acting. Rudyard Kipling was a magician who could make animals talk and live, and the glowing Indian scenes made a contrast to our rather humdrum childish lives. Northiam was sunk in a country peace which is unimaginable now. We were ten miles (or thereabouts) from Robertsbridge, the nearest station, and were driven to and fro there when we came and went to the village, in rain or shine, in an open wagonette. Nothing happened much except the usual country things, and so we were forced to make our own amusements. One of the bitterest disappointments in my life was when a circus came to the village. It rained in torrents, the circus packed up and went away. We had talked, planned, and dreamed of nothing else for weeks, and our real despair when we realised that the performance would not take place, I shall never forget. I have seldom since then felt that particular blank unhappiness and disappointment descend upon me. My Aunt Katherine Lyttelton[1] took us to the village shop and bought each one of us a small toy. I hope we appeared grateful for her kindness, but I always looked at my toy with a sick aversion, as it reminded me of the circus I hadn't seen.

Our field of books, as I have said, was a narrow one. Though we always studied the French language, we were never allowed to read French books except Halévy's *Princesse*, *Mon Oncle et mon Curé*, and the *Malheurs de Sophie* books.

As far as we were concerned, French literature was brooded over by darkness, and lit with flames of immorality. As I soon learned to read French as easily as English, it was a great temptation to me to pick up any French novel I saw on a table.

Our elders handled this whole subject of what we could or could not read with a good deal of clumsiness. My father's attitude was a liberal-minded one, and he thought that it would not hurt any child to be let loose in a library to read anything on the shelves. He gave me *Peter Simple*, and I read and reread it. It was an odd choice for a child, as the incidents described in it were not those of the drawing-room or the vicarage. (I would not dare to read it again; I liked it so much, and might now think it less good.)

My mother, who was always rather afraid of what other mothers would think and say, was much stricter than my father, and I got into great trouble when I was growing up, because I once lent a book of Whyte Melville's to my cousin Alice Grosvenor.[2] I liked it and had seen no darker implications in the story. My aunt had the very unpleasing habit of opening her daughter's letters, and she pounced upon mine recommending this book. My mother was not really so shocked at my having read it, as she was annoyed at the *faux pas* I had made.

[1] My mother's youngest sister, Katherine Stuart Wortley, who married the Honble. Neville Lyttelton.

[2] Daughter of the 2nd Lord Ebury; married Ivor Guest, afterwards Lord Wimborne.

Reading

If our elders had let well alone we should probably have taken no harm from any book. But they showed a great lack of judgment in this way, and prohibitions in the matter of reading only served to make us scrutinise every sentence closely, in any book that fell into our hands. Sometimes, I am sorry to say, we read books before we had asked permission to do so. If we had not been made to feel that books were dangerous, we should have run through them without trying to seek for underlying meanings. Children on the whole have healthy mental digestions, and can assimilate a very varied diet of reading without coming to any harm.

I was a "real reader" because I seized every book that came to hand and having read it remembered the contents. I read straight through Scott and Thackeray (I couldn't bear Dickens until I was much older). But I didn't only like adventure. I liked quiet books about children who went out to tea and who skated on the village pond. Love stories bored me, and I have never been able to get through a girls' school story, though I knew *Tom Brown's Schooldays* and *Stalky and Co.* almost by heart.

In my youth we had wonderful magazines, the best of which was *Aunt Judy*, in which appeared some of Juliana Horatia Ewing's stories as well as miscellaneous articles on history, poetry, flowers, and objects of the seashore. Mrs. Ewing was an admirable writer. She wrote, to my mind, the best children's short story ever written, *Madam Liberality*, and *Six to Sixteen* for older children has a real living charm about it. All the girls in her books had hobbies, and showed a laudable passion for learning about the habits of fresh-water fish, and at the seaside collecting sea shells and seaweed. Mrs. Ewing herself had a passion for seaweed in all its varieties, and when she was ill her friends would send her parcels of it to cheer her and give her pleasure. Natural history could then give amateurs a pleasant sense of pioneering, and they sometimes made useful discoveries.

My Great-uncle Stephen Lawley (my grandmother's brother), finding me sitting under a cedar tree on the lawn of Ripley House struggling to model a profile of a goddess in red wax plastered on to a board, with a pointed wooden tool, patted my shoulder and remarked, "That's right, child, make your life out of little things." Little in that case was the right word, and I soon abandoned my futile efforts to do bas-reliefs with an alacrity which showed clearly that my heart had never been in this form of art. But Stephen Lawley and Mrs. Ewing would have agreed about girls being always occupied.

As well as *Aunt Judy* we had *Saint Nicholas*, an American magazine admirably produced and written, and full of first-class stories. I loved American books and was specially devoted to *What Katie Did*, *Little Women* and *Jo's Boys*. *The Wide World* I found dull, but I fell on Fenimore Cooper's tales with avidity. I took scalping, tomahawking, and the blood-curdling whooping of Red Indians just as much in my stride, as I had earlier taken the Border raids and forays.

I should like to record how thankful I am that I read all Jane Austen's books in my youth. My mother just told me that they were delightful and amusing books, and I devoured them one by one, before the spate of essays, criticisms, erudite comments, and fanciful sequels of her books were in evidence. I have always loved Jane Austen. Her freshness never palls and I can read her unselfconsciously, without asking myself all the time how she compares with other writers; and I can now see fine shades in her writing which I did not see in youth. I have a strong feeling that if Jane Austen were to return to life on this planet, she would be astonished and scandalised by a great many well-meaning books written about herself and her work.

Now the whole picture of children's reading has changed. One of my mother's taboos was *Adam Bede*. I was not allowed to read it until I was about sixteen. A few years ago I was giving away the prizes at a large school, and to a tot whose head hardly surmounted the table behind which I stood, I handed *Adam Bede*. I am amazed when I go to libraries to find that quite small children have read *The Thirty-Nine Steps* and *Greenmantle*. My husband certainly never intended them as children's books.

If children are allowed now to read books which are too advanced for them, we on the other hand were too much kept to childish things when our minds were able to grasp something more adult. I must, however, say that we were encouraged to read history, and I should imagine that we read a great deal more of it than children do to-day, to our lasting benefit.

My parents subscribed to the *Yellow Book*, and I read it from cover to cover, when I grew up, some years after it had been published. I liked a story called "A Captain of Salvation" by an extremely young and quite unknown author named John Buchan, and Henry Harland's stories of the Quartier Latin were my delight, and I read them over and over again. The *Yellow Book* was a grand browsing ground for a reader, and it gave me many happy if sometimes puzzled hours. I was asked the other day if I remembered anything about the literary movements of the 'nineties. Alas! I do not. I never heard Oscar Wilde's name mentioned till after I was grown up. My mother was asked by one of her grandchildren to tell them about the "Naughty 'Nineties." She replied austerely that she had never noticed anything particularly naughty about them, and certainly no echo of literary naughtiness penetrated into the high and narrow walls of our schoolroom.

2

WRITERS AND ARTISTS

I WELL remember my first encounter with a writer. I can see a lamp-lit room, with my mother sitting behind a tea-table, and a stocky man with strongly marked black eyebrows, who had just risen to take his leave of her. I was a small child, but I received, even so, an impression of a sort of electric vitality filling the room. My mother told me afterwards that the name of her visitor was Rudyard Kipling. He often came to see her when he was living in London, but when he went to live in the country their friendship lapsed. I only met him once again at a luncheon party in Oxford, in 1918, I think, when I received again an impression of crackling vitality.

Rudyard Kipling's reputation has waxed, waned and waxed

again through the years, with the general run of people, although discerning readers have never wavered in their allegiance to the best of his work. My husband steadily read and reread his books, and at Ottawa they were often in his hand. I remember John saying that Kipling would be remembered as much for the stories and poems in *Puck of Pook's Hill* and *Rewards and Fairies* as for anything else he had ever written.

My next literary contact was a meeting with Frederick Anstey, the author of *Vice Versa*. I can now, alas! recollect nothing about it, except the fact that he and I solemnly bicycled together around Hyde Park. He was clad in a tweed suit, and was extremely kind to a tongue-tied little girl. He said nothing memorable to me, and afterwards when I wished to boast of my meeting with him to other children, I could think of nothing to say. But I went on reading his books with increased delight.

One of the most interesting things about looking back over the years is to try to see who were the people one met in childhood or youth, who really counted because of the influence they had on one's later life. My mother made friends with Elizabeth Robins (Lisa we all called her) and she entered vividly into our childish life. She had made her name as an actress in Ibsen's plays, and we revered her as someone who really *was* on the stage. Compared to the cinema-bred children of to-day, my sister and I were utterly unsophisticated, and had seen practically no plays at all, beyond one or two performances of Shakespeare and some kind of innocuous play about fairies. But the thrill of meeting a real live actress was great. Lisa was very kind to children, and early in our acquaintance asked us to go to tea with her, and showed us a sofa on which she lay when she learned her stage parts. This gave me a slight shock, and an insight into the drudgery and hard work behind the glamour of the stage. My eyes grew round and I drew a long breath, as I realised that acting would be no career for me, as I have seldom, in spite of repeated efforts, been able to learn anything by heart.

Lisa imported a vivid interest into our lives and stirred the air in our rather dull schoolroom. We had never encountered an American before we met her, except our Aunt Sophie

Grosvenor, who often indulged in a wildness of statement which made conversation with her a perpetual excitement; but she was a New Englander with a stern Puritan code of manners and behaviour. Although Aunt Sophie was an artist in the everyday things of life, her clothes were exquisite, and I have never tasted more delicious food than she provided; she liked (we thought) dull and conventional people.

Lisa Robins came from the Southern States of America, and she had that warmth and richness of enthusiasm which Southerners possess in such a marked degree. Her small face, her long-lashed, vivid blue eyes and tawny, chestnut-coloured hair made her remarkable in any company. We all loved her, and I shall always be grateful to her for opening my eyes to the priceless gift of enthusiasm, for helping me not only to feel that so much in life was worth while, but to know that I could be enthusiastic without being absurd.

Lisa had run away from home as a girl to go on the stage in America, much (I have heard) to the dismay of her family, who held old-fashioned views about the stage. She came to England to act in London. I am not sure when she started to write books. Her first novel *The Open Question* was widely read and discussed, and later she wrote a book describing the Klondyke gold rush called *The Magnetic North* which has remained a classic of that episode.

My mother and sister and I spent a summer in Florence, and my mother wired to Lisa, who had been ill, asking her to join us there. Lisa's illness had been costly and she hesitated to embark on further expense, so she said she couldn't see her way to coming. My mother wired again from Florence, and it came through to Lisa with the words "Let not scruples hinder you from coming." She came, saying that she could not resist the Elizabethan ring in the wording of the telegram.

We stayed in the Via Venezia, in a flat entirely carpeted by matting, where we were fed like fighting cocks by an Italian cook who had married an Englishwoman. We learned to speak some Italian and got to know intimately the galleries and churches of Florence. My mother was copying a picture—she did this beautifully—and she was an admirable guide for sightseeing as she had a great knowledge of pictures and architecture.

We were made to study the history of the different periods of architecture, and if we sometimes felt a little tired of art I do not think we showed it. When I accompanied my mother on sketching expeditions to the Villa Lemi outside Florence, I sometimes dropped my paint brush and stared at the landscape, feeling my inadequacy as a painter in watercolours; with the result that my mind enriched itself with the beauty of the scene though my technical skill did not improve. The rigorous training in looking at pictures which my mother gave me, has stood me in very good stead all through my life.

Various people came to visit us in our flat at the Via Venezia. One of them was Mrs. Fleming, Rudyard Kipling's sister. Her husband was stationed in India, and she hated the life in that country. She adored Italy and said one day that she would close her eyes on her return to India, and paint the walls with roses and cypresses. I being literal-minded said, "Does she paint?" and was told "No," this was merely a manner of speaking.

I sometimes went with my mother and Lisa to see Vernon Lee.[1] She lived in a small villa with a shady garden. She was an intimidating person, who always seemed to be expecting one or other of the company to say something brilliant. I felt that I was there on sufferance; the young were apt to feel that in those days. Vernon Lee said one day that she thought the bird whose head was carved in the top of my parasol looked rather intelligent. I replied that I expected that its wits had been sharpened by long sojourns at the Lost Property Office in London (I was always a notorious umbrella-loser). This remark of mine (which I quote with diffidence) was considered promising, but whether the promise was ever fulfilled I cannot say. Years afterwards I read Vernon Lee's books, when I was writing a book about Charlotte of Albany,[2] and I was surprised by their lightness, and the way they recaptured the charm of Italy in the

[1] Vernon Lee was the pseudonym of Violet Paget, writer of fiction and aesthetic criticism.

[2] *Funeral March of a Marionette*, by Susan Buchan.

eighteenth century. Vernon Lee had always seemed rather governessy to me, and I took up her books expecting them to be full of information, but heavy and probably dull.

We spent a great deal of time at Bellosguardo, where Lady Paget[1] had a villa, which stood on a shelf commanding a magnificent view. She herself was an intimidating old lady, a creature of strong prejudices, with decided views on how people should conduct their lives.

One of her articles of faith was vegetarianism. Lady Paget was the most militant vegetarian I have ever met. The first time we lunched with her she fixed my sister and myself with a stern glance remarking in her slightly guttural German voice, "I have ordered some meat for the young ladies." We would gladly have sunk into the earth, but as it did not obligingly open to swallow us up, we helped ourselves to slices of flannelly veal, and ate them in stricken silence, feeling both coarse and carnivorous.

Another of Lady Paget's crusades was on the subject of clothes for older people. She maintained that as you advanced in life you must wear only white. It was a doubtful tenet to hold as far as the majority of the elderly were concerned, but it suited her very well, as she was still extremely handsome in a Roman matron sort of way. She wore a shady white hat and long dresses, and, if the weather was cold, an ample woollen cloak tightly buttoned up to her neck.

She took us one day for an expedition into the country in a wagonette. In a narrow lane we met a cart to which was harnessed two stout bullocks. Both vehicles stopped dead, neither would give way. The driver of the bullocks, and the friend who sat beside him, volubly protested that there was no room for the two vehicles to pass each other. Lady Paget thought otherwise. She first scolded the driver of the cart, and then asked him in stately Italian to give her pleasure by measuring the gap between the cart and the high bank at the side of the road.

This produced a kind of mild tumult, but Lady Paget got her way, as she produced a long piece of tape from somewhere under her white cloak. She made the measurement which proved that

[1] Widow of Sir Augustus Paget, *née* Countess Walburga de Hohenthal.

there was a foot or more to the good, and the wagonette, half up in the air and sliding like a crab, somehow scraped and bumped its way past the cart.

The bullocks appeared uninterested, and the men shrugged their shoulders, obviously saying over and over again to each other that the *Forestieri* were even madder than they supposed. Lady Paget looked majestic and triumphant.

She comes rather by chance into this chapter dealing with writers, as she wrote an imposing volume of memoirs which described all the well-known people she had met.

"Shall we be in it?" I asked my mother. "I think not," she replied drily. "Lady Paget is only interested in famous people."

We lingered on in Florence until the late summer; it became very hot, and even the clamorous flower-sellers grew languid about bargaining, and flung bunches of flowers into vehicles which passed them. (We had no carriage of our own, but we took public conveyances with a certain recklessness.)

I had never seen fireflies before that summer in Florence, and fireflies at night are one of the most completely satisfying sights in the world.

Lisa was dining one evening at a villa outside Florence and my mother let me go off in a little *carozza* to fetch her back. The luminous deep blue sky, the dark roads, the fields over which the fireflies danced a brilliant ballet—all these I can see on dull days if I close my eyes even now.

One last reminiscence of Florence. An Italian friend of Lisa's volunteered to take Marnie[1] and myself to a circus. It was a very hot evening, and we sat in an arena open to the sky which looked like dark blue velvet. The circus followed the usual pattern of circuses, until it was announced that Signor —— would bring on his famous band of performing sea-lions and they then flopped into the arena raising clouds of sawdust.

Musical instruments were thrust between their flippers and at a signal they started to bang on them. I have rarely seen a sight in which pathos and comedy were so equally blended. The bewildered expression on the sea-lions' faces, the series of per-

[1] My sister, Margaret Grosvenor, who married Jeremy Peyton-Jones.

functory and discordant sounds they made, moved us to tears, but also, alas! to laughter.

My sister and I said goodbye to our escort at the foot of the stone staircase which led up to our apartment, and after we had thanked him in choking voices, we rushed up stairs, the walls resounding with our merriment. But we were ashamed of ourselves, when we thought of what those sea-lions must have endured, and to this day "How sea-lion" is a family expression when anything crops up in which pathos and comedy are mixed together.

I have never been to Florence again, but I have talked much of it with my son John, who was there in the war. I would love once more to see the frescoes in the Riccardi Palace and to go up to Bellosguardo, and to see the fireflies dancing in the corn.

There have recently been in the newspapers some articles about Mrs. Humphry Ward[1] on the centenary of her birth. I was so glad to read them, but the writers did not do much more than give a short account of her various activities, and these achieved nothing very much in the way of bringing her to life. I should like to write a few words about her here, as her kindness to me was very great. She was an extremely interesting person, and I am grateful to Fate that I knew her in my youth. The Wards' country house, Stocks, near Tring in Hertfordshire, was a pleasant, pretty, red-brick house. It stood in a valley, while on the hill opposite was a small house called Stocks Cottage, at the edge of a lovely beech wood on the slope of the hill, and there we walked and picnicked when Mrs. Ward lent it to us for a holiday.

In my recollection I always seem to see Stocks filled with people who came and went. The Wards made their house a meeting-ground for all conditions of men and women—in fact, Stocks was the ideal country house, overflowing with life, so that those who liked conversation and discussion could enjoy them with ease and pleasure. Mary Ward's interests were so various that the chances were that you would meet someone who was engaged in running a settlement in the East End of London, a well-known French writer, or a member of *The Times*

[1] Mary Ward, writer of novels and philanthropist.

staff, or the editor of a newspaper. Arnold, the Wards' only son, who had just come down after a brilliant career at Oxford, organised cricket weeks which the young people enjoyed very much.

Our hostess worked all the time, and I was conscious, in an awestruck sort of way, of the fact that she did her writing somewhere upstairs, and was never interrupted while she was working, an indulgence rarely granted to any member of the female sex who is a writer. Her charming and unselfish daughter Dorothy ran the house and was beloved by everyone for her gentleness and humour. Janet, her sister (who afterwards married George Trevelyan) and I read aloud to each other, and she introduced me to Matthew Arnold's poetry by reading me *The Church of Brou.*

Mary Ward always gave me a reassuring sense of being on the top of everything she did, of knowing exactly what she wanted to do, and of enjoying doing it. I remember in my youthful uncertainties and perplexities envying her for this. Her life was full of interesting events over which she seemed to have complete control. The Wards' family life was a very happy one, and they spread this happiness widely to include many people.

Mary Ward had a pleasant speaking voice. She had soft and pretty grey hair parted in the middle, a large nose, and dark eyes which sparkled with zest and enthusiasm. She wore long dresses and large wide-brimmed straw hats. Her conversation was serious on a high intellectual plane, but her vital interest in all the subjects on which she talked, prevented her from being overly highbrow or dull.

Her books were eagerly read both in England and America. People bought them and clamoured for them at circulating libraries. It is difficult to say why her books, which were so much read, discussed, and admired by men and women in many ranks of life, are hardly read at all to-day. Mrs. Ward could tell a story, and that is by no means a universal gift. She could make her characters talk interestingly, and her books must be now a rewarding study to students of social history, as Mary Ward was nothing if not accurate in her portrayal of people and their background.

But her creative power was not great and her characters did not emerge vividly from their surroundings. I would say that she was more at home in her approach to history and philosophy, and in her welfare work at the Settlement which bore her name, than in the fiction by which she earned both fame and money.

When I think of the many maladjusted and frustrated people I have known in my life, I look back to Mary Ward, with her immense powers of work and her integrity of mind, with a sense of refreshment and comfort.

My parents had made a great friendship with the Hugh Bells. Hugh Bell was an ironmaster at Middlesbrough and they lived at Redcar, and also in London. Florence Bell was the writer of many books, one of which, *At the Works*, describes in a very human and charming way the lives of the men and women at her husband's works. This book must be of great interest and value to writers who wish to know about labour conditions at the time when she wrote. She had two daughters with whom we spent some part of our childhood. Hugh Bell's daughter by his first wife was Gertrude, later to be well-known as an Oriental scholar and archaeologist.

When I was a child, Gertrude Bell alarmed me and my sister. She had a way of putting us through our paces over our talents and enthusiasms, and we felt horribly small and childish. After my father's death she came out to Dresden to be with my mother, and her tireless love of sightseeing exhausted my anaemic adolescence. We were on bicycles one day and I was suddenly seized by one of those gales of giggles which have been my bane all my life. This particular paroxysm was so severe that I tumbled off my bicycle, cannoning into Gertrude's back wheel. She reproved me severely but kindly. I remounted my bicycle, but from sheer nervousness my giggles returned, and the incident was repeated. Gertrude's sharp reproof rings in my ears now. I felt that she loved my parents dearly, and put up with their children for their sake.

Her amazing thoroughness and powers of concentration fill me now with endless admiration, and she is one of the few women who have made a permanent mark on history. She liked my husband, and when they met they became absorbed in talk about archaeology and Eastern questions. Aunt Mamie, who, though unlike Gertrude except in concentration of purpose, was devoted to her, was reduced almost to despair when Gertrude started to write books about Arabs. My aunt had nicknamed dwellers in the East comprehensively "Obadiahs," she could never distinguish one from the other. She threw up her hands and said, "I've had to listen to Anne[1] for years about Obadiahs and now Gertrude has taken to them. I can't bear it."

Gertrude Bell had the pleasant feminine trait of liking nice clothes. She dressed admirably, and gave (I should say) a great deal of thought to the matter. I can remember her at one of her stepmother's parties armoured in a sheath-like evening dress of solid black sequined material, her red hair beautifully dressed, looking at me a little pityingly and saying, "What did you do in the war, my dear?" (Two of my sons had been born during the war years, and I had worked pretty steadily at war jobs, as well as the difficult housekeeping of the day, but I could think of nothing to say.) She looked at me and said thoughtfully, "People can do such *dull* things in wars."

Her own war record has passed into history. Gertrude had the steely efficiency and genius for concentration which was shown in another field by Florence Nightingale. I always think that far the best study of her is a short but very vivid one by Vita Sackville West.[2] When I want to remember Gertrude (and all my youthful fear of her is now merged in admiration), I reread this passage and feel glad that I knew her long ago.

Another writer whom I knew in my youth was the Scottish poet and historical novelist, Violet Jacob. My mother and I were in Egypt staying with my uncle and aunt when Violet's husband, who was a soldier, came to Cairo with his regiment. She accompanied him from India. My mother and aunt liked her, and she came often to General's House.

Violet had published a small book of poetry, which made her a little suspect to the military society of Cairo. But her charm

[1] Her sister-in-law, Lady Anne Blunt, who was an Oriental scholar.

[2] *Passenger to Teheran.*

and beauty and aptitude for getting on with people helped her to live down even poetry. My mother and I were staying with Percy Machell[1] in his house on the banks of the Nile. There was a dinner party, to which the Jacobs came, and I disappeared into the garden and sat on a wall with a young man, talking and looking at the moonlit scene. We stayed doing this for a long time, and when we finally returned to the drawing-room my mother and Violet looked extremely exhausted, after a long evening of making conversation to various not very interesting dinner companions. I remember Violet's quick, sympathetic smile when the young man and I, conscience-stricken at having stayed away so long, came in together.

Violet had one son, whom she loved with all the depth of an imaginative and passionate nature. When he was killed in the 1914 war a spring in her broke. She never wrote a long book again, and turned to writing poems in the Scottish vernacular. *The How of the Mearns* goes on being recited and read, especially in Scotland, where poetry plays a real part in people's lives.

Her two novels, *The Interloper* and *Flemington*, should live while people read historical novels. They are full of incident, and have passages in them of exciting beauty. John thought that the incident of the Cadger's Ride in *The Interloper* was as good as anything Scott ever wrote, and he admired *Flemington* so much that he wrote to Violet Jacob an exceedingly long letter in his own hand, a thing he seldom did to anyone. His handwriting was cramped and small, and very hard to read. I asked Violet if she had enjoyed getting it. She replied, "It was the most wonderful letter I have ever had, and I was so proud that he liked my book so much." Then she added, "It took me three days to decipher it, and then I read it again, and then I pasted it into my own copy of the book."

Our friendship with Violet Jacob continued in the way a real friendship continues, with occasional letters even if we had few meetings. The last time I saw her was in Wales in a grey-walled country house near that demi-paradise, the Hay Valley. The house I remember was full of flowers, especially of beautiful pale

[1] An official in the Egyptian Government.

mauve single scabious. She had grown a little deaf, but her zest for life was as great as ever—and the keen edge of her sense of beauty had never been blunted. She showed me some of her paintings, which were charming in design and colouring. After her husband died she lived in Scotland in the countryside she loved best, and from which she had so long been exiled.

We did not know many artists when we were children. But William de Morgan and his wife were friends of the Lovelaces and I saw them from time to time, though they were hard-working artists with little time for social life.

They lived at The Vale, King's Road, and I recall that it was heavy with Virginia creeper, whose strands had to be parted to allow passage into the house, where a pleasant shabbiness reigned. There was a gentle charm and philosophy about William de Morgan and he was a delightful talker. I remember we once went to see them in Florence one evening—in their little apartment. Conversation turned on life after death, and William de Morgan said, "I should like to be a speck somewhere in the sky when I die, a speck with intense perception."

When his first novel, *Joseph Vance*, came out and brought them affluence, their life became like something in a fairy story. Their friends rejoiced as they watched this delightful elderly couple basking in a glow of prosperity. Mrs. de Morgan was able to hire a carriage, in which she drove about London, and to wear the rather sombre purples, greens and peacock-blue clothes which were then to be bought at Messrs. Liberty.

My mother had a great deal of help in her painting from Lord Carlisle,[1] who was a constant visitor at our house. George Carlisle was a patron of the arts, and himself painted both landscapes and portraits. He was a small, slight man with a delicate, sensitive face and finely cut features. He looked sceptically at the world, and had a quietly sarcastic turn of phrase. I possess two of his paintings, one a sketch of a shepherd driving a flock of sheep through a field near Naworth, the other a villa in the South of

[1] George, 9th Earl of Carlisle.

France, white against blue sky and standing in pale pink blossom. The two pictures make a pleasant contrast, the fields near Naworth in shadowy neutral colouring, and the southern villa blazing in a hard glare of sunshine. He painted a portrait of my mother which I never greatly liked; he managed somehow to make her look hard and a little sly, which it was not in her nature to be.

We saw something of both the Burne Joneses and Poynters. I always wondered why Sir Edward Burne Jones looked so cheerful and Sir Edward Poynter so sad.

I haunted exhibitions of pictures in those days, and warmly appreciated those by Rossetti which glowed with romance, and I was much *froissée* by my uncle, Archie Stuart-Wortley, who was a painter of meticulous realism, remarking irritably, "Nonsense, child, you can't really like him. Why, the man couldn't draw, and he couldn't paint."

My mother and I went once to see G. F. Watts. We were taken to his studio by Mrs. Prinsep. We went first to her house, where I was childishly entranced by being shown a small square aperture in the hall which opened and shut. I was told that when the house was built, they had commanded the architect to make this tiny door (which worked on a hinge) in the wall so that their beloved dog could open it and come in and out as he pleased. I thought this going rather far just to please a dog, but it made far more impression on me than did the venerable silver-haired artist in his skull cap in his studio full of tall canvases.

3

EGYPT

MY uncle Reginald Talbot[1] had been appointed as General Officer Commanding the British troops in Egypt. When I was growing up my mother and I went to Cairo for a winter. Life there, my aunt wrote, was gay, and I must have new clothes. My clothes up to then had been quite neatly made, but were

[1] Son of the 19th Earl of Shrewsbury.

more for use than for smartness, and I secretly longed to wear black velvet, rather than the homely blue serge considered suitable for the schoolroom.

I remember as a near-tragedy a biscuit-coloured confection, which suffered a sad decline when I was taken to tea in Cairo with Lady Wingate, the wife of the Sirdar.[1] I was very shy and, I fear, clumsy, and upset a cup of tea down the front of my dress. I wilted with embarrassment, as all polite conversation had to be suspended, while I was taken upstairs for the damage to be repaired, and my crumpled skirt bore witness for the rest of the visit to what I had done. But a spoilt dress was only a small incident in the life of colour and romance to which I found myself transported.

The voyage out was beautifully fine and warm. There were several charming young men on board, and I saw Stromboli at night lit up by little necklaces of fire running down from its volcanic cone. When we landed at Port Said we went to a large house with a handsome lady who was a friend of my aunt's and the wife of an official. I drank orange wine and sniffed the scent of the East. *The Arabian Nights* seemed to be opening to me in that very modest first glimpse of the world.

This experience and those which followed it can only be savoured in extreme youth, because youth lives in its own climate, and so everything sets a youthful imagination to work. Memory has played a very neat trick on me. While I was in Egypt I moved in a sort of heady excitement of dances, picnics on the Nile, walks in moonlit gardens, rides in the desert on donkeys which were swift in running, but came suddenly to a halt, lunches, dinners and visits to mosques. The young man of the moment occupied my thoughts; though I had grown up as a serious reader and a fairly serious student of history, I seldom opened a book, and my thoughts dwelt on a gay and frivolous level. But the curious thing is, that now when I think back to my youth in Cairo, I remember the *décor* but not the actors in my particular drama.

Nearly all the young men who were my companions and

[1] Lieutenant-General Sir Reginald Wingate, K.C.V.O.

partners were killed in the 1914 War as colonels or majors, or
have gone out of my ken, and their good spirits and charm are
like a glow on a far-off horizon. Now I only recall the kites as
they dropped from the sky, giving a strange, shrill cry; and that
Cairo was full of delightful sounds and sights. Donkeys brayed
continuously, always sounding very angry about something, and
when one got into the heart of Cairo the water-sellers called
their wares, and vendors of necklaces of shells and beads shrieked
continually, "Berry sheep, berry sheep" (very cheap). I never
tired of this endless, vivacious scene.

Shopping in the bazaars in Cairo was always a joy—in fact,
the only perfect type of shopping I have ever known. We drank
delicious (if gritty) cups of Turkish coffee and watched shafts of
sunlight strike into the dusty half-light of the bazaar, and touch
the carpets and necklaces we were being shown with a lingering
light. Time did not seem to exist, neither did it appear to matter
if you bought anything or not.

Outside the wall of the front garden of General's House went
an incessant stream of camels, going where from, and to where,
I have no idea. They padded along looking supercilious, though
what the poor beasts had to be supercilious about I do not know,
as they strode past with heavy bags of green stuff strung on either
side of their humps.

My aunt was frightened of horses shying and rearing, and there
was nothing her carriage horses disliked so much as the sight of
a camel. It is hard to avoid camels in Cairo, and when she drove
out to leave cards on the wives of various officials in the afternoon, the drive resolved itself into a struggle both for the coachman to steer his horses past the camels without any untoward
incident, and for my mother and myself to converse so interestingly, that my aunt would not notice the aversion of her two
quadrupeds to the camel population.

Lord Cromer[1] lived at the British Agency on the banks of
the Nile, at the end of the same street (if you could call it a
street, composed as it was of large houses in shady gardens). He

[1] Sir Evelyn Baring, afterwards Lord Cromer, British Consul-General in
Egypt.

stands out in my memory as a figure of intense interest and importance. He was short, stocky, red-faced, and wore pince-nez. He disliked anyone who havered and was lengthy in explaining things to him. There were tales that people who were spreading themselves conversationally, would be cut short by a firm hand thrust decisively at them, and that they were out of the room and down the steps of the Agency before they had time to realise what was happening to them.

My Uncle Reginald Talbot was a sensible and efficient soldier and got on well with Lord Cromer. My aunt[1] was beautiful, charming, and vague in the extreme, and it was a tribute to her charm that Lord Cromer came so much to General's House. "Your aunt is the most undecided person I have ever known," he said to me once with amusement in his eyes.

If you asked Aunt Margie anything, she would drop her hands and say, "Oh, I don't know. I must consult ——." Blank always being of the male sex. Those women who had grown up in the Victorian age always considered a man's judgment on any subject to be of paramount value. It was a saying among us that my mother and her sisters would ask any man—say, a plumber who happened to be in the house—about the political situation, rather than seek the opinion of a highly intelligent and well-educated female relation.

Aunt Margie's beauty and gentleness and complete lack of conceit disarmed criticism of her vagueness, although I am certain that the edgy and suspicious diplomatic corps who formed a large part of Cairo society were completely baffled by some of her wilder sayings. She often talked her thoughts aloud with no regard for her audience, and they undoubtedly read meanings into what she said that she had never intended. The British officers and their wives also found her hard to understand, but her endless kindness, when anyone was ill or in trouble, endeared her to them so much, that they let deeds talk, not words.

She was a keen gardener and directed the Arab gardeners in General's House gardens with skill and energy. For some reason she looked after two pelicans (lent to her, I suppose, by the Cairo

[1] My mother's sister, *née* Margaret Stuart Wortley.

Zoo). They barged about, doing the garden no good. In fact, one of them constantly entangled himself amongst the rose bushes, and bled profusely over the garden paths. But garden-lover as she was, she continued to keep the pelicans in the garden. It was a charming study in incongruity to see Aunt Margie, slim and beautifully dressed, holding in a gloved hand a small fish, while the pelicans hurried clumsily towards her with their grotesque beaks widely open.

Lord Cromer was a widower when we first knew him, but on our second visit to Cairo he had recently married the beautiful Lady Katherine Thynne.[1] She had a charming simplicity of character and an unconventional outlook. Like my aunt, she loved gardening. Lord Cromer said that when she lost her wedding ring in the garden she bought another, lost that, and now bought them by the gross in the Bazaar at Cairo to replace any that vanished.

Looking back, I can well understand why she loved her garden. The Agency garden sloped down to a wall beyond which flowed the Nile, and above the wall winged feluccas (native sailing boats) turned from gold to amethyst in the evening light. Over all the walls of the garden hung curtains of purple bougainvillæas, mixed with fleshy, bright orange flowers whose name no one ever seemed to know. It is always a delight to plan a garden which is already framed in a lovely setting.

British prestige was very high in those days in Egypt. Lord Cromer was officially the adviser to the Khedive, but really he ruled Egypt with an admirable staff of men who got things done, and showed British administrative talent at its best. Many of these men became well-known later in other spheres of work. Great Britain had given an equitable government to Egypt, and though the *fellaheen* attributed their improved circumstances directly to Allah, it can only be said that in Lord Cromer Providence had a marvellous instrument ready at hand.

Lord Cromer was one of the greatest administrators the British Empire has ever produced, and history will do him justice and establish him firmly in his niche. Anyone who wishes to know

[1] Daughter of the Marquis of Bath.

the historical background against which my girlish adventures were set should read *England in Egypt*, by Sir Alfred Milner (afterwards Lord Milner). The whole story is set out there with a charming lucidity and humour. It was not a new book when I read it in my youth, and now I think it has perhaps been forgotten. I hope not. I would recommend it to anyone who is anxious to understand, or write about, a complex period of history. The whole tangled story of the British in Egypt in those days is brilliantly done with complete knowledge and admirable powers of exposition. I myself am not attempting to write history, and am only trying to indicate what it was like to be young in Egypt in the early years of this century. Life for me was enchanting, and people were kind and indulgent to youth.

One more recollection before I close this chapter. It was announced that the Austrian Archduke Franz Ferdinand was coming to Cairo on an unofficial visit with his wife. He had married a lady not of royal blood, and although he had not renounced his own succession to the Austro-Hungarian throne, he had done so for any sons he might have.

I was all agog to see the Archduke and his wife, and my chance came when I was invited to go to a ball at the hotel where they were staying. It was usually considered unsuitable for me to go to hotel dances, but this time I was allowed to go to join a reel danced by the officers of a Scottish regiment. I went, full of excitement, as I pictured the Archduke's wife as a mixture of Venus and Pallas Athene.

While the Archduke and his wife watched the kilted dancers and the girls with their pale, long dresses, their faces were completely impassive, and my romantic dream vanished. She was far from slim and had a round, stolid face under a pompadour of lifeless brown hair, while the Archduke, too, was no Adonis, with his stiffly brushed-up hair and solid figure. Grouped round them were various aides-de-camp with their wives. All the men were in the attractive Austrian uniforms and the women wore fine jewels, but they looked as static as a group of waxworks.

Who could have foretold that in a few short years not only

would the two principal figures in the drama die violently, but that their passing would sound the death-knell of the world as I knew it in youth.[1]

4

SOME COUNTRY HOUSES

AS staying away in country houses formed a great part of my life when I was young, I feel that a description of this almost forgotten mode of existence may not be out of place in this book.

We used in August and September to go regularly for what was called "a round of visits." We did not stay quite as long at each place as people did in earlier days, but it was not on the other hand worth while to go for too short a time.

A journey meant looking up a lot of cross-country trains in *Bradshaw*. We usually had several changes which, with my mother's spacious ideas about luggage, needed a great deal of planning. There was no such thing as going by a fast train to a junction and being met there by a car. We bumbled through the countryside hour after hour, waiting at branch line stations, while my mother would murmur to herself that she wondered if the whole thing was worth while. Our mountain of luggage would certainly have intimidated any modern porter.

We were usually met by a smart brougham and a luggage cart, and to the best of my recollection we invariably arrived at a country house about tea-time. We were sometimes late for tea, found our hostess already comfortably ensconced behind a massive silver tea urn and fell to eating paper-thin bread spread with home-made butter, and scones with delicious jam.

My mother's maid unpacked her clothes, and mine were usually left to the housemaid to deal with. Clothes were stowed away in great wardrobes and roomy chests of drawers. That benefit of civilisation the coat-hanger had not yet arrived on the scene,

[1] The Archduke Franz Ferdinand and his wife (*née* Countess Sophie Chotek) were both murdered at Sarajevo in June, 1914.

and we hung up all our dresses on hooks in the wardrobes. My mother invariably took her winter and summer clothes with her, as she distrusted the British climate and its vagaries. She continued this habit after 1918 when she came to stay with us at Elsfield for only a few days. My aunt's Irish butler once praised the smallness of my own luggage saying, "It's not like Mrs. Grosvenor's. By the Holy Saints, I thought hers was like elephants stuffed with stones."

My mother had been born in the era when you took sketching materials, and a great many heavy London Library books, as well as clothes. She usually also had an embroidery frame, and as she was often studying a language, primers were added to everything else. There was always also a bundle of rugs containing a stick, an umbrella and a parasol, as well as a sketching easel, also a basket which held endless medicine bottles.

After the war, I often exhorted my mother in the strongest possible terms not to bring so much luggage; porters were then (as they are now) hard to come by at Oxford Station. But I was always made to feel a hard-hearted brute, when the weather, just I felt to spite me, would change suddenly from hot to cold or vice versa. My mother would then say wistfully, if it was hot, "I wish I had brought my garden hat," or if cold, "I am feeling very chilly without my third woolly coat," because like many of her contemporaries she lived weighted down by heavy garments.

It must be remembered that on a round of visits we dressed for dinner every night, and that we could not be expected to come down every evening in the same gown. Our long and ample dresses took up a great deal of space in our large, dome-like trunks, which were made of the strongest and most durable leather.

My earliest country house visit was a frightening one. I must have been very small at the time—when I was taken to stay with the Carlisles at Castle Howard in Yorkshire. It was a vast house, and I seemed to be constantly lost. I wandered in a sort of bad dream, crying for my nurse and my parents, among the legs of endless gilded tables in wide passages hung with tapestries and pictures. I was much more alarmed by the house than by its mistress, the formidable Lady Carlisle, who struck terror into many hearts by her rudeness and her bludgeoning methods of argument; and I remember that I boldly presented her with some mushrooms I had found on one of the lawns, while I clung to my father with my other hand.

My next country house visits were to Wortley Hall, near Sheffield, the home of my mother's cousins Lord and Lady Wharncliffe.[1] Wortley Hall was the *Stammschloss* of my mother's family. It was built in 1800 and inhabited from then onwards by the Wharncliffe family. The family fortunes were based on coal, and a faint greyness hung over the countryside from the town of Sheffield and its surrounding collieries. Sometimes when we gathered flowers our fingers would become a little black. The house was well situated on a hillside, the garden sloped upwards from the back of the house, and the property included farms and moorland.

In the house there were many fine pictures—my mother pointed out to me the portrait of Lord Bute (George III's unpopular Prime Minister), who married my ancestress Lady Mary Wortley Montagu's daughter. He was painted in flowing robes wearing the Garter, by Sir Joshua Reynolds. There was also a picture of a swarthy ancestor who fell fighting at Marston Moor. This interested me more than the portrait of Lord Bute, but the picture I liked best was a fancy piece by Evelyn de Morgan representing a young lady tied to a rock, while a young man is actively engaged in slaying a dragon. The family cherished the legend that a Miss Wortley had been carried off by a dragon at some unspecified and early date, but had been rescued by a young man, who afterwards married her. With childish boastfulness, I resuscitated this dragon legend whenever other children made me feel inferior. It was not everyone, I maintained, who had a dragon in their family. No one could better this story; the dragon took the trick every time.[2]

There was a walk we took sometimes along the Wharncliffe

[1] We gave them the courtesy titles of "Uncle Edward and Aunt Susan."
[2] There is a ballad about the dragon of Wantley in *Percy's Reliques.*

crags to a minute stone house,[1] and we approached it through a wood which reminded me of Merlin's wood with its gnarled and ancient trees.[2]

We children lived in a wing of the house which must have been built either for Aunt Susan's baby (who died in infancy) or for an earlier generation of children. In all the rooms of the house I remember huge coal fires which never seemed to collapse or to go down in size or heat. It was easy for a child to make up Hans Andersen-like stories while staring into their glowing depths.

One of our greatest delights at Wortley was a visit to the stables on Sundays. Everything was in exquisite order, and a plate of carrots was handed to Uncle Edward, for us to give to the horses. But we had been through this performance before at Moor Park, and the object which really riveted our attention was in a glass case—we were never allowed to touch it, but we peered into it and saw a model railway engine with two railway coaches attached to it, standing on miniature railway lines. The Wharncliffe coachman had made this in his spare time. We had never seen a streamlined mechanical toy of this kind before, and this miniature of the train in which we travelled from London to Sheffield was to us little short of a miracle.

Aunt Susan and Uncle Edward were people whose mode of life and outlook could only have existed in the late Victorian era. They moved with majesty and had rigid and exacting standards of behaviour and conduct. Uncle Edward, who I remember best in country clothes which suited him perfectly, held conventional views about men's dress. About a year ago, when I was looking through some family letters, I found one to my mother, written when she became engaged to my father. Uncle Edward was very fond of my mother, and his letter is a model of polite disapproval under a veneer of congratulation. He wrote: "I have not yet met Mr. Grosvenor, but I saw a young man at a ball in London who was wearing a black tie. I asked who he was and was told that this was Mr. Grosvenor." He went on to say that he hoped she would be very happy. Luckily for us, on

[1] The lodge at Wharncliffe Chase.   [2] Wharncliffe Chase.

66

further acquaintance he liked my father very much, and forgave him an occasional eccentricity in dress.

Aunt Susan was charming to look at. She had a small face with neat, pretty features; her golden hair always shone with endless brushing, and was coiled in a knot at the back of her neck. She wore in the evenings the heavy, important-looking silks and patterned brocades then in fashion, with grace and dignity.

I remember her doing (I was going to say acres of) needle-work. Many of the curtains in the big windows at Wortley were embroidered by her. She had the humorous detachment and philosophy which was the gift of so many of her contemporaries. Her life at Wortley cannot have been an exciting one. Uncle Edward was a very good shot, and they were invited to all the largest and most imposing shooting parties. "I sometimes feel," she once said to my mother, "that for part of the year I am married to a gun, not a man."

She had, of course, her compensations. Wharncliffe House still stands in Curzon Street, and they went there for some months every year. I remember it vaguely as imposing but dark, and that there was a conservatory which I should have liked to explore, but which somehow was out of bounds.

Before I leave the subject of Wortley, I would like to recall a strange little episode. We children were told that mummers were coming one evening to sing and dance. What that meant we had of course no idea, but we were allowed to sit up later than usual when they came, and that in itself gave us keen pleasure. We assembled in a room with a stone floor. In came a party of men dressed entrancingly in short coats with bright coloured patterns on them, and long dark trousers. Their leader wore a large rabbit-skin cap with a small rabbit's head in front.

The songs and dances were charming, and the men's faces interesting and serious. These mummers were the real thing, and their dances were not inscribed on any printed page, but had come down to them from their forebears. Harry Cust, who was married to our cousin, Nina Welby, was there, and he took down songs and stories from one of the mummers. The man was surprised and reluctant, but eventually told him in scraps and fragments something of his own and his friends' mumming activities.

One of the songs began pleasantly with,

> Tantiro Tantiro, the drums they do beat,
> The trumpets they do sound upon call,
> Methinks music's here, some bold captain's near,
> March on, my brave soldiers, away!

I remember now Harry Cust's face alight with interest as he talked to the captain of the mummers. He wrote an article about them in the *Pall Mall Gazette*, which he was then editing for Waldorf Astor. I do not know if it interested people. It should have, because it was brilliantly written, but the cult of English folk lore had not dawned then on the horizon of the intelligentsia.

I remember in a childish way being interested in the mummers, realising dimly that they came from an alien world, quite different to the ordered and staid mode of life in that staid and orderly household of Wortley Hall, and that they represented something historical, rough, and elemental.

We stayed often with the Brownlows all through my childhood and youth at Ashridge Park, near Berkhampstead, and at Belton near Grantham. Lord and Lady Brownlow[1] were (except for my uncle and aunt, Margaret and Reginald Talbot) the handsomest couple I have ever seen. They were both very tall and had a kind of impressive magnificence of air.

Lady Brownlow's clothes never conformed to any special fashion. She wore in the evening brocaded dresses of dark ruby colour, or white patterned with gold—and flowing dresses in the day-time. She had a delightful character and was kind and generous to an extreme degree; and was always willing to lend her attention and to open her purse to any tale of distress, though there was a slight lack of coherence in her mind, and she might get the whole thing a little out of perspective. Her thoughts

[1] Adalbert, 3rd Earl Brownlow, married Lady Adelaide Talbot.

dwelt in the immensities, and she sometimes gave forth cloudy and sibylline utterances at odd moments. There is a story that when she was staying at Hatfield, Lord Salisbury was preparing to go out one afternoon, and while he was looking for his mackintosh and goloshes in the hall she pounced upon him saying, "Do please tell me, do you *really* believe in the immortality of the soul?"

To my mother and myself she was invariably kind and welcoming, and I can recall endless happy days at Belton and Ashridge. The beech woods at Ashridge were a marvel of beauty in the spring and autumn. They had a romantic quality denied to the house, which was very large and very Gothic, though it had a dignity of its own. It possessed a chapel and an endless chain of imposing rooms. At some time on a journey abroad, Lord Brownlow had made friends with a German professor whom he invited to stay at Ashridge. The professor arrived at the door, and gazing with stupefaction at the huge pile of masonry, rang the bell and enquired in which part of *this village* Lord Brownlow lived?

Ashridge had tall windows, and the rooms hung with Italian pictures were graceful and charming. The gardens were splendidly kept by an army of gardeners. Lady Brownlow often sent my mother flowers: roses, magnificent in colour and scent, and carnations whose great heads nodded on their frail stalks. When I married, my mother asked if she might have "a few flowers" from Ashridge to decorate our house at 30 Upper Grosvenor Street. A mass of vegetation arrived resembling nothing so much as Birnam Wood coming to Dunsinane. There were vast branches of beech, as well as heaped baskets of lovely flowers.

In my much humbler way, I am myself a gardener, and I can appreciate the endless labour and skill which was spent in growing these perfect blooms. To grow flowers so that each blossom reaches perfection is one of the finest of fine arts.

Belton was more compact and beautiful than Ashridge, and the house was full of lovely tapestries, pictures, and fourposter beds hung with embroidered curtains. I always enjoyed staying at Belton for the Grantham ball, and have other recollections of days when we were alone with our host and hostess, and when I was allowed into the library and spent most of my time there, until someone reminded me that exercise was essential for the young, and I was dragged out for a walk or a bicycle ride. We often stayed at Longford,[1] near Derby, which was architecturally most beautiful. I remember it as a house which was full of light and space and tall eighteenth-century portraits. It belonged to Henry Coke,[2] Lord Leicester's brother, who had married Lady Katherine Egerton, my father's cousin. Cousin Henry Coke was intellectual, sardonic, and extremely deaf. He carried a strange, snake-like tube in his pocket with a cup-shaped attachment, into which his interlocutor tried to talk. When the conversation bored Cousin Henry, he most disconcertingly snatched the tube away, and replaced it in his pocket.

His wife had a talent for acting, and her daughter, Sybil Crutchley, was one of the moving spirits in a permanent amateur company called the Windsor Strollers. I loved my hostess, and we went for many walks together, clad in mackintoshes and thick boots, along the muddy Derbyshire lanes.

I fear that I avoided Cousin Henry and his ear-trumpet, as I was too shy to shout my very ordinary remarks into it, while his whole family listened and laughed amongst themselves.

I am sorry for this now, as Cousin Henry (if I could have penetrated the wall of his deafness) was an extremely interesting person. He had made a journey in his youth to a remote part of South America and written a book about it, and his caustic comments on people and events were well worth hearing. I possess a lot of his letters to my mother written in a high strain of romantic friendship. Cousin Henry was completely careless of what people thought of him, and it was said that he had done most eccentric things, like ringing the bell at 2 a.m. in a French hotel, and demanding cold artichokes to be sent up to his room. I am sorry that I did not talk to him more about the part which the Cokes had played in English history. They were a very long-lived family and had many astounding links with a distant past.

[1] Longford Hall, Brailsford, Derbyshire. [2] Honble. Henry John Coke.

Life at Longford had a charming simplicity about it, and the
days went by quietly. The meals were plain, and there was a
pleasant shabbiness about the bedrooms. There was no formal
kind of entertainment, and we went out for long walks which
led to nowhere in particular, or for a drive in a pony cart. Longford was situated in what was called in those days "the depths of
the country," and was the sort of place about which one of my
aunts said obscurely, "It was so quiet that one might meet a
unicorn in the road." Sometimes we walked stolidly over wet
fields and along lanes, our objective being a small village shop
where huge striped peppermints were sold. They were admirable
in themselves, but it proved impossible to lever them into our
mouths, and they had to be taken home and hammered into
splinters before we could eat them. The days passed in an ordered
procession, and in the evenings we played cards or parlour games.
No one at Longford asked me to play tennis, for which I was
thankful, but we played croquet, the only outdoor game I like
or can play at all. Otherwise I read in a browsing kind of way,
and my mother sketched. I remember the days at Longford with
a pang of nostalgia for the time they gave me to read and to
think. When Sybil Crutchley was there, life became gayer and
more animated. Sybil always reminded me of a very dark and
pretty squirrel. She had the sort of charm that would have wiled
a bird off a tree and her acting was exquisite.

In the early 1930s I had a glimpse of Longford. I was helping
to run a settlement in South Wales, in a mining area. I went
with Helen Brown and Ruth Egerton to visit clubs and settle-
ments for unemployed men and women. We were on our way
to see a settlement at King's Standing. We drove past Longford,
and I had a moment of sorrowful regret as the Cokes were dead,
and the house which looked so lovely, and so much as it had
done in my youth, had passed into other hands.

Escrick, near York, belonged to the Wenlocks whose family
name was Lawley, and who had come from Shropshire. After
one of the Lawleys had married a Yorkshire heiress, they settled
at Escrick in the flat plain of York. Escrick was a severe-looking
Georgian house, which was often a target for disparagement from

the artists and wits who were glad to go and stay there. One of them said that it looked like a cigar box with windows, another that Escrick never disappointed you, as it was always uglier than you remembered it. Actually it was a dignified house both inside and out, but it might have been a little dreary and dispiriting to live in, had it not been for the personality of its hostess.

Constance Wenlock[1] influenced me very much, and I still often think of her. She had a sympathy with young people and an eager interest in them, which was rare in her generation. I only wish that I could talk to her now. I am certain that if she lived in these restricted days, she would somehow find a way of making life charming for herself and other people.

Constance Wenlock always dressed in a style of her own, and wore bonnet-like hats which charmingly framed her small and lovely face. Her clothes were long and graceful, and in no current fashion. Her mere presence in a room spread gaiety like ripples round her in every direction. She became, as she grew older, stone-deaf and often ill. She carried a small ear-trumpet, which really was shaped like a trumpet. She draped a tiny black veil over it and held it up to you with a quick charming gesture, so that no one felt any embarrassment in talking into it. She made her deafness completely unonerous to other people, and when not listening to someone talking into her ear-trumpet, she sat with a look of secret happiness on her face. As she was small in stature her trumpet usually had an upward tilt.

After her family and her friends, her two passions in life were painting and gardening. She rose at a very early hour in the morning, in order to paint a sunrise, or some effect of early morning shadows on grass. Her paintings are interesting studies of fine shades of colour in landscape. The figures of people which she put into them were a little weak and lifeless, but her ability to interpret a moment of light or shadow in town or country was considerable.

Her powers of work were astonishing. She resembled Edward Lear in this. He also rose at an unearthly morning hour, and the volume of his work is enormous. But Lear did sell at any rate

[1] *Née* Lady Constance Lascelles, married Beilby, 3rd Lord Wenlock.

some of his pictures, and held yearly exhibitions either in London or abroad. Constance Wenlock showed her work only occasionally to her friends, and though some of her pictures hung on the walls of her house, no one was made to feel that they need either notice or comment on them.

The more one knows about the Victorian upper class, the more it is clear that they took literally the Biblical command not to bury any talent they had in a napkin. If they had talents they used them, and used them to the full, and they worked at their artistic pursuits with an industry and a concentration which leaves a later generation gasping for breath. Moreover they enjoyed themselves, which is more than many people do nowadays.

Fairy godmothers in their busy occupation of attending christenings give out a strange variety of qualities. I have often wondered, in my journey through life, at their niggardly ration of the more graceful qualities to the babies to whom they present gifts. But sometimes one of them is in a sunny mood, and she gives a child the gift of delighting in beauty, and the power to spread it all around him or her—Constance's fairy godmother was generous in this respect.

After her death a correspondent contributed a letter to *The Times* about Lady Wenlock: "Her letters, which were voluminous and full of her own peculiar charm, could hardly take the place of her conversation, but she wrote them, by a happy chance, upon the typewriter. And as she regarded all machines as live things, diabolically inspired, an unexpectedness, differing from, but almost as delicious as that of her spoken words, was imparted to what she wrote. No inanimate object was inanimate for her; each had a will of its own—and the typewriter had the strongest of all. She herself enjoyed its amazing exploits almost as much as any of her correspondents."

The contribution of the country house and its inhabitants to the intellectual and political life of the nation was, I am certain, very considerable.

Many people who write of country houses to-day, write about them without having in the least idea what life in them was like. It is not hard to assemble the facts, to describe a house, to say something about its owners, to enumerate the servants, horses and carriages possessed by any particular landowner. But it is very difficult to evaluate the cross-currents of talk, the importance of some public man meeting someone whom he wished to talk to, the conversation and the ideas which germinated in brilliant talk.

Beatrice Webb made a devastatingly dreary remark to the effect that she "thought nothing of a week-end in a country house which did not end in the formation of a committee." This showed at any rate that she considered that people who went to country houses would be valuable on public bodies.

In the ideal country house—I will not say which it was, as I am making a composite picture of several in my mind—there was space and beauty. There were gardens formal and informal, where under shady trees the guests could discuss books and politics, or wander in the green undulations of a park. Many of these discussions made the fame and fortune of a book, and helped to shape the policy of a political party.

In a gathering of people selected by a really clever hostess, there might be one or two Cabinet Ministers who welcomed the opportunity of quiet conversation, or there might be a Viceroy or high official from a far-off corner of the Empire, anxious to make someone in the government of the day realise a little more the difficulties of a particular experiment that Britain had delegated to him to carry out. These parties often included a diplomat home on leave, a painter, and almost certainly a musician who played to some of the company in the evenings. Besides these eminent people there was usually a sprinkling of women famous for their beauty or wit, or both, who either gave the conversation a sparkling turn, or were wise enough not to interrupt good talk, and who accordingly sat looking statuesque or flower-like. Fussy and boring people were not asked to these parties; they were "swept up" into large entertainments given in London.

Two people of the opposite sex who were known to be attracted to each other were often asked to the same country house party, and most great men had an Egeria to whom they were platonically or passionately devoted. Romantic friendships flourished, and scandal was always circulating either openly or in whispers about them.

Country house gatherings as I remember them in my young girlhood never lacked every kind of interest and drama. A girl who was admitted to one of these very adult gatherings was expected to sit silently by while her elders talked. I liked this very much, and quietly watched the faces of my fellow guests. I also feasted my eyes on the loveliness of my surroundings, and looked at the pictures, the cabinets, the long straight curtains shutting out the cold and darkness of a November afternoon. The shadowed corners and angles of the walls held cabinets full of china, and there were beautiful objects on tables and mantelpieces. Pictures of all kinds made a background to the human beings gathered round the fire on chairs and sofas. Not that everything in a room in a country house was beautiful. These houses were a delightful mixture of all sorts of things. But there were also delightfully fubsy objects which a parent or grandparent had thought desirable and charming.

I remember a room in a country house where the magnificent fourposter bed was ornamented with priceless and beautiful hangings. Near to it was a small round table covered by a faded cotton velvet cloth trimmed with very ordinary lace. The Victorians had no snobbery in the way of wanting to make their rooms look like furniture shops. They liked a mélange of everything, and thought it homely and pleasant. They would have been chilled and repelled by a pale coloured room with a few widely spaced pieces of good furniture, in a taste so restrained as to be almost invisible.

I have drawn a picture of the kind of country house party which was the *fine fleur* of a civilised society. But it would be idle of me to suggest that this pattern was to be found everywhere.

There were houses, to which one went usually for family reasons, where the hostess was dull, the host, if possible, duller, though there was always a gleam of hope in a youthful heart that one of one's fellow guests would have some entertainment to offer. But the days went slowly past, and the evenings more slowly still. Yawns were hard to suppress, and glances at the mantelpiece clock which was usually surmounted by gilded figures looking very somnolent themselves, became more and more frequent. However, the young people could go away and stifle boredom by noisy games on a billiard table.

Shooting parties were, I thought, extremely dull. I have never liked seeing birds shot, and the weather was usually wet and cold so that one could go out very little. In the evening, the men were half asleep after a busy day of sport.

I was asked the other day if I really wore a tea gown at tea-time. My answer was no. Married women wore elaborate lace affairs, in a sense the ancestors of the "house gown" of to-day, but the girls wore a summer dress or a "best dress" of some kind. (There was a wide gulf fixed between our best dresses, and our everyday clothes.) We wore rather heavy and, I should say, looking back, rather dull tweeds in the day-time. The sort of tweed suit which is now the fashion, made of charming material and colour, had not yet dawned on the horizon.

Some of the nicest times I ever had in a country house were when I was the sole guest after a large party had left. Then the house and stables settled down to their regular routine, and I joined in the normal life of a family and became one of a little, busy, private world enclosed in a park wall or fence.

I would give anything now to be able to recapture the atmosphere of a country house. In the foregoing pages I have written mostly of large houses which were the setting of the fashionable world of politics and sport. But when my thoughts fly back to my country house visits, I remember with most pleasure the smaller houses where I stayed. They varied between Elizabethan, seventeenth, and eighteenth century, Victorian Gothic, and other modes of architecture. In all of them, life moved at an easy tempo, and our greatest excitement was a sale of work or a garden party in the neighbourhood. Our greatest anxiety was that the weather should be fine for these activities, as well as suitable for the crops.

Garden parties were not really amusing affairs for the young. They were mostly composed of the ladies of the neighbourhood with a sprinkling of elderly clergymen. The guests stood about under spreading cedar trees and ate heartily of cakes, ices and lemonade, all of the first quality of excellence. If there was not much to amuse in these gatherings, there was a quiet charm about them, and a dignified acceptance of the fact that life in the country was bound to be at the best a bit humdrum.

I should like to be able to recapture the sounds of a country house standing in miles of quiet countryside. These particular sounds have gone, and are replaced by the grinding noises of machines in the sky, and on the farm.

I love to remember long afternoons merging into quiet evenings, when the big ormolu clock ticked loudly in the hall, a hay waggon lumbered along a distant lane, the voices of the hay-makers came faintly on the breeze, and a door opened and shut somewhere in the house, giving a faint jar to the silence.

Time was our great talisman, though we did not know it then, and we who were young perhaps should have made better use of it. I am glad I tried to struggle (on one of those afternoons which I describe) with the *Pensées de Pascal* and one of Hegel's works (in translation). These and other difficult books toughened my mental muscles, though I probably understood very little of what I was trying to read.

5

INVITATION TO THE VALSE

PEOPLE sometimes ask me what the balls in the early nineteen hundreds were like. I will try and recapture a little of their atmosphere.

The balls at the great London houses were entertainments which had their own majesty and splendour. Your feet had hardly carried you over the red carpet outside the house, when you found yourself in a room to the right or left of a great staircase.

Your hostess's maid and a co-equal whom she had summoned

and who was generally a lady's maid in the household of another member of the family, took your cloak from you. Removing your cloak in those remote days needed patience and skill, as cloaks were long and voluminous. There was usually a smallish gilt-framed looking-glass on a table, but the girls could only take a hurried and furtive glance at it, since they dared not push into the orbit of the chaperon who was at that moment examining her appearance.

There was no question of making up one's face. We were supposed to have done the whole work of making ourselves presentable before our own looking-glasses at home. The *croupier's* words: "*le jeu est fait, rien ne vas plus,*" seemed made to fit our situation.

I well remember the agonising suspense while I stood getting my long gloves smoothed down, while my mother talked, endlessly as it seemed to me, to a friend, and the thudding sound of a waltz began overhead. It was not so much anxiety to join in the dance that I felt, as the acute fear that all the nicest partners would be snapped up before I got upstairs.

We had no dance programmes; they were considered, as one of my uncles said, "rather second circles," so that the memory strain was great, and cutting dances an easy thing to do. Programmes, however, were always given out at Hunt Balls in the country, and were agreeable and often long-cherished souvenirs.

When you had managed to detach your mother from the cloakroom, you emerged into the hall feeling nervous and apprehensive. A footman escorted you both up the stairs and handed you over to a butler who called out your names with ringing distinctness at the top of the staircase. You found yourself on a landing and, after shaking hands with your host and hostess, looked at the groups of people of all ages. The married ladies were gay with tiaras and other jewels, the unmarried girls were more plainly dressed and wore no jewels except for a small pearl brooch, or a modest seed pearl necklace. My own mother was shy, and was not really a great support to me, though she had many friends who were kind to us both. She took her place among the dowagers who lined the walls of the long stately room where dancing was in progress. Running the gauntlet of the dowagers was a formidable affair for any girl. If you were elderly and powerful you could be rude. It is no baseless legend that chaperons stared through *lorgnons*—and *how* they stared— causing alarm and despondency among those they stared at. The evening dress one had put on with so much care, and looked at with modest pride in one's bedroom glass, seemed now all wrong, and any good looks or social graces one possessed shrivelled away under the raking searchlight of the *lorgnons*, which pursued me through the room to see what Caroline's and Norman's girl was like.

I often felt worthless and out of place, and any charm or usefulness I had in daily life, was vanishing like a wreath of mist in a chill wind. It must be said in justice to the past, that many dowagers did not abuse their position by staring unkindly at débutantes, and even found partners for girls who did not know many people. But the serried ranks of dowagers sitting bolt upright on gilded chairs or sofas round the room underneath glittering chandeliers intimidated much bolder spirits than mine.

All the same it was this alert audience of critical older women that gave a big London ball its authority and its atmosphere. They got tired, those poor chaperons, because, like the Frog Footman, they were there on and off till morning. The faces of the straightest-backed and most armour-plated among them grew paler and more drawn as the evening wore on. But they conceived it to be their duty to sit up in order to chaperone some young relation, and sit there they did. The one break in the evening was when they were armed into supper by an elderly beau of former days who usually arrived late, or by their host, or by some important man who had been told off for this purpose. Sometimes driven by hunger, they had several suppers during the evening.

Supper would either mean a delicious consommé and some fruit and coffee, or a more substantial meal of quail or a cutlet in aspic, followed by an ice. The chaperon and her escort talked about politics, on which they were usually very well-informed, hunting and farming and other country pursuits. Then came some gossiping remarks about their fellow guests at the dance. They were related probably to at least half the people in the room, had known the others well from childhood, and could talk in well-informed terms about the interplay of attraction and counter-attraction, which ran like an undercurrent below the shining surface of the party.

Those women who lived in a sort of goldfish bowl by reason of their beauty and worldly importance, knew that a battery of discreet glances was fired on them at a ball. Did Lord Beckley[1] (a Cabinet Minister) spend most of the evening with Mrs. Marston? It was well-known that he was devoted to her, and that his wife bored him. Mrs. Marston was lovely and could be both witty and amusing. Somebody had whispered at a ball the week before that Lord Beckley was transferring his interest to Mrs. Woodeaton. Conjecture was in the air, and, if not much was said aloud, excitement mounted on the chaperons' bench. Mrs. Marston was in great good looks, they thought, and she seemed to be amusing the great man as much as ever.

Then Mrs. Rycote was having supper with Sir Denzil Islip. That affair had gone on for so long that it had almost become respectably dull. One glance reassured the onlookers that there was nothing new there to interest them. Mrs. Rycote and Sir Denzil were talking placidly about Ascot, or Goodwood, and were eating a hearty supper without self-consciousness.

Then thoughts which had turned away from the young people focused themselves upon a lovely débutante in cloudy white muslin with a red rose. "She really is very pretty," thought the mothers with a pang for their plainer daughters. "Who was she dancing with?" "Oh, Lord Studley." He was known to be flirting with a married woman. Oh, those young married women, what pirates they were. Having achieved matrimony they should really become respectable and stay at home.

On the chaperons' bench, heads delicately crested with diamonds came closer together, and a long whisper ran along the sofas and gilded chairs on which they sat, as the pretty girl and her partner whirled past them looking happy.

[1] I have taken the names of the villages near Elsfield.

"*She's* not here yet," murmurs one chaperon to another. "We shall see when she *does* come." The young married woman enters with a partner and joins the dance. She is beautifully dressed and sparkles with diamonds, and has the poise and self-possession which would be lacking in a young girl. The two couples meet and greet each other, and the married woman looks curiously at the girl and everyone of the quartette is a little tense.

Then the débutante and Lord Studley spend a good deal of the evening together. It is obvious that they are much attracted to each other. His married friend leaves the ball early to seek in future other conquests, and the girl and the young man may eventually marry. Or this may not happen; I have known the story end either way.

The young people who were actively engaged in dancing had eyes that were less keen than the chaperons. The time passed in a flash, and their immediate interest in each other was paramount in their thoughts, but at supper they looked and watched also.

Some of the chaperons had not only daughters but sons at the ball, so that their interest as well as their anxieties were twofold. Sons were notoriously less meek than the daughters of those days, so that the chaperon who had her precious son at the ball, looked less often in his direction although her anxiety about him might be far greater.

Lady Wolvercote's thoughts might run somewhat on these lines: were her son's thoughts turning perhaps towards marriage? If so, would the girl of his choice be good to him and to any children they might have? Would she look after the house, and rule the servants wisely and kindly, and see that the clergyman did his work properly, not too High or too Low in his views, and also look after the tenants and help with the old people on the estate? Would she spend months in the country cheerfully and without complaining, or would she always want to be out hunting, and spend too much of the family money on horses; or want to be too often in London, or, worse still, go to Paris, and reduce the family dignity by taking no interest in the place or in country pursuits? Would the girl her son chose (whom he might be dancing with at that moment) take her rightful place in society and keep up the family position and prestige, and some day take her appointed place in the long line of Lady Wolvercotes, putting duty and responsibility before pleasure, and thus keeping the family together? In a society based on landed property these thoughts were inevitable, and it cannot be too much stressed that the hosts and guests who met together in a London ball spent a large part of their life in rural surroundings, and had some of a rural realism in their thoughts about marriage.

No doubt towards morning some of the chaperons must have felt lightheaded from hunger and fatigue. A cup of soup and some fruit, and even a small quail, do not last for ever, but their iron social training enabled them to sit bolt upright without yawning, and to say a graceful and composed goodbye to their hosts. Their daughters went down the stairs behind them wondering whether they were in for a fearful scolding for having danced so often with a highly ineligible young man of great charm.

One of the strangest things to look back to was the unblushing snobbery of even the nicest people. My mother and aunts often told me that there was far less snobbery and much more simplicity in the London social world in their youth. She and her sisters, as my aunt Mary Lovelace described to me, were always short of money, but one of them was a reigning beauty who had refused to marry a duke, and they all had their admirers. They wore inexpensive tarlatan dresses and painted and repainted their kid ball slippers to match them. But this did not prevent them from being asked to the most exclusive parties in the great houses. When I grew up, society was expanding and becoming more moneyed, and a less rural standard was creeping in. Society, so called, had also become much larger. Some eldest sons of peers married Americans and other heiresses, which buttressed the family fortunes at the cost of bringing in much higher standards of smartness in clothes and equipages. We had travelled a long way from my grandmother in her rusty black bonnet and cloak.

Looking back at London balls and entertainments I am not concerned to praise or blame them. I should be delighted if I could be wafted back to a great ball in a great house and smell again the scent of the splendid roses and malmaison carnations, brought up from the host's gardens and greenhouse somewhere in the country, and to hear the sound of the band playing a waltz or the lancers. There was something heady and exciting in the scent and the sound. But truth compels me to say that often I did not enjoy myself quite as much as I should have liked to do, though I did on the whole always find a lot of pleasure at a ball.

Anything that is set in a rigid pattern, as social life was in my youth and in my mother's youth, has hard edges on which human beings can cut themselves, and a girl who "came out" in London learned a good deal about a harsh and capricious world. She learned to swim in a rough sea with sunken reefs. Having had a dull and quiet upbringing in nurseries and schoolrooms, she would often thankfully have bartered the chance of enjoyment at a ball for a schoolroom supper and an early bed and a quiet time reading *Vanity Fair*. But Vanity Fair of a different kind was her portion, and to be seen at the right balls her duty.

We early learnt the useful lesson of just how kind or unkind people can be. All young people have to learn this lesson. Boys, and now girls, learn it at school, but we had to learn it when we grew up, and we learnt it thoroughly and quickly. On balance I would say that people were more kind than unkind.

Hunt balls were different—they were part of our winter social life. We drove there in a station bus from the country house where we were staying. When we arrived at the Corn Exchange in the local town where the ball was held, we felt the throb of excitement at the thought of seeing so many unknown and possibly thrilling people.

To our hostess, or any other chaperon, these dances must have been pure purgatory. These heroic women sat bolt upright hour after hour while cutting draughts from every direction assailed them. They had, of course, some pleasant conversations with country neighbours, and took part in a set of lancers, and were whirled in a wild polka by a red-faced Master of Hounds, who danced with more vigour than accuracy, on a floor from which rose clouds of chalk. But brain anaemia from cold and weariness set in long before the young people were ready to go home.

It was always a distinction to be asked to dance by a young man in a so-called "pink" coat, and the girls at Hunt Balls always tried to wear colours which did not clash with the scarlet of their partners' coats. I always enjoyed Hunt Balls; they had more gaiety and spontaneity than their London counterparts. I loved the drive there and back between hedges and with glimpses of the sleeping countryside beyond them, and perhaps a sickle moon pendant in the sky over the side of the hill.

One ball I went to took place in Banbury, and I stayed at Broughton Castle, which had been taken on a lease from the owner, Lord Saye and Sele, by Lady Algernon Gordon-Lennox. Banbury was then only a name to me in a nursery rhyme. I little knew how well I should get to know the real Banbury, and that years afterwards it would mean memories of pleasant meals, nice shopping and friendly meetings.

Broughton Castle is famous for the fact that the Roundheads met and held a conference there in a high upper room at the beginning of the Civil War. It is beautiful and romantic, but I was nervous at night, and my horror was great when I found myself in a bedroom at the end of a great echoing corridor. Part of the wall of the bedroom consisted of two square wooden panels. They could be opened, and from them you looked into the chapel. One of these panels suddenly swung back in the middle of the night letting in a draught of icy air. Nothing more happened, and the incident was unexplained. I can only imagine that intimidating things often happen to easily intimidated people.

6

THE SERIOUS SIDE

IN this final chapter to my foreword to youth, I have tried to write about a few matters which should not be neglected in a book which deals with the points of view of various people.

My father was an agnostic and so was my mother. They did not go to church, but they had a stern code of ethics, which included the Christian virtues of unselfishness, kindness, and generosity to anyone who was unhappy or poor. To be an agnostic in a powerful clan of church-going people was to set oneself apart, and my father suffered a great deal of criticism from members of his family, some of whom had never given themselves the trouble to think out their beliefs as he had.

Owing probably to the influence of my two devoutly religious grandmothers and to a natural bent toward religion, I have always subscribed to Christian tenets, and been a church-goer; but I can deeply sympathise with those who honestly wrestle with doubt, and who suffer unpopularity and criticism because of this, as my father did.

My mother and my aunt Sophie both said that at Moor Park the question asked on Sundays was, "Where will you go to church?" not "Will you, or won't you, go?" One nearby church to Moor Park was High and the other was Low, and you attended whichever service suited your preference. The church and its hierarchy was discussed keenly, and held an important place in people's thoughts and conversations. Nowadays, when you stay in a house for the week-end, people often do not attend church at all, and the subject is never mentioned. Sunday is treated exactly like a weekday, even in houses where the host and hostess are people of proved integrity.

The church was far more powerful in those days than it is now, and religion held a more central place in the minds of men and women. In many country villages the little churches are now practically empty, the bells ring and the village people go by on foot or on bicycles, not heeding the call to attend service. Yet we are told, and it is true, that there is a very real interest in religion, a longing for spiritual help. Certainly the services broadcast by the B.B.C. are eagerly listened to by many. It is the church-going habit I knew in my youth which has completely lapsed. Men and women will go to church if they wish to, but not otherwise. A fine and sympathetic preacher, a man who reads the service beautifully, may fill a church and keep it filled. If he leaves the parish and someone comes who has not got these gifts, the church will empty again.

The Lilac and the Rose

I have sometimes been asked the question, "Were the people you knew when you were young more spiritually minded than they are now?" A very hard question to answer. I would say tentatively that men and women realised more than they do now that the things of the spirit were the most important part of life, and that, if they disregarded them, they were turning away from God and trying to solve their difficulties only on a material plane. They realised, at any rate, something of what they were losing.

I think that respectability played some part in the regular church attendances of yesterday. In a village it was distinctly respectable to go to church, and the church porch, after the service, was the meeting place for people of all conditions of life; also a place for conversation and the exchange of views. I remember when, as a Londoner of many years' standing, I first came to the country, I asked a village woman her opinion of another inhabitant of the small village in which she lived. I had not enough knowledge of rural life to realise the unwisdom of such a question, and when she replied quite simply, "I have never spoken to her in my life," I felt very much put in my place. But, pondering the remark afterwards, I understood the meaning of what she said. The church attendance in that particular village was very poor. The country bus and the Women's Institute had not yet reached it. There was no meeting ground where people could get to know each other. The church was no longer the centre of the village for religious and social purposes.

I feel a deep sense of loss when I think of the days when religion filled such a great place in life, and, if it was discarded, was done so with deep searchings of heart and a high seriousness. Nowadays, I feel sorry for the many people I meet who are anchorless and rudderless, and who unconsciously long for the things of the spirit, without having the strength and discipline of mind to go out and find them.

My mother, although she did not go to church herself, encouraged me to do so, and, when the time came for me to be prepared for confirmation, she arranged for this to be done by Canon Scott Holland.[1]

[1] Canon of St. Paul's Cathedral; writer of many books.

The Serious Side

As we grow older, one of the sadnesses which beset us is that of lost opportunities. I made all too little of the privilege of talking to Canon Scott Holland. He lived in a small but lovely house under the shadow of St. Paul's, and we sat in a long room at the back of it, looking out on to a garden where sunshine and shadow played on a lawn and some trees. He gave me lessons by myself, and he must have found them very heavy going, as I was consumed by shyness and did not respond quickly or, I fear, intelligently. I dreaded going to these talks, I can't now think why, as he was extremely patient, and he had the kind of enthusiasm which should have appealed to a young person. Canon Scott Holland was an ugly man with a pale face and dark hair. He was seldom still, and threw himself into his chair and out of it with great rapidity. There was not a trace of primness or stiffness about him. Sometimes he asked me to write a short essay for him, and I blush, even now, to think of the jejune stuff I laboriously turned out for his reading. He wrote me long letters in one of the most illegible handwritings I have ever seen. Most of them I failed to read, even after faithfully trying to do so.

I don't know why this whole episode was so unsuccessful. I regret it deeply, but all my life long I have been glad that I knew Canon Scott Holland. At any rate he showed me that saintly people need not be stiff and starched, but could be both saintly and cheerful. That much I did get from knowing him. I think that perhaps living in a household where Christianity was not much spoken of made me feel that the whole phraseology of the church and of religious belief was embarrassing and difficult to understand. I should like to think this, to excuse myself for my stupid self-consciousness and lack of response.

When I was confirmed in St. Paul's Cathedral I experienced an uplifting of heart and spirit and gained a sudden vision of spiritual happiness. A vision which, though sometimes clouded, I have never lost.

It was perhaps inevitable that I should start my career in welfare work under the ægis of Mrs. Humphry Ward, and I started to go weekly to the Passmore Edwards Settlement (now called the Mary Ward Settlement) in Tavistock Square, to help with dinners for crippled children. The cripples were pathetic and charming and I liked them, and handed them their dinners with zest. Then I felt the need for doing something which would teach me more about the conditions of the poor, and I went several days a week to the Charity Organisation office in Baker Street. My father had known and admired Sir Charles Loch, the founder of the C.O.S., as it was called. It filled a place as a co-ordinator and clearing-house for charitable effort. The emphasis of the C.O.S. was on extremely careful investigation of problems, meticulous case-work and filing of information. Anyone who applied to the Charity Organisation Society for help had to give their reasons for asking for assistance. Begging letter writers abhorred the C.O.S. In those days they showed real artistry in pulling out every stop of pathos. The C.O.S. investigated all letters which were sent on to them, and showed that the writers usually made a good living out of exploiting other people's feelings.

Beggars abounded in London in those days, and the C.O.S. held the widely publicised opinion that the donation of a coin only did harm to the recipient by encouraging further begging, and that it also discouraged the beggars from making any effort to find work. They said, severely, that if anyone genuinely wanted to help someone else, they should not thoughtlessly give away money, but put time and trouble into learning the whole history and background of the seeker for alms. Then they should try and help them to get into a more secure way of life. Many people paid lip-service to this view, while continuing to hand out coins and do nothing more; but others sought the advice which the C.O.S. readily and intelligently gave. This often resulted in a great improvement in the circumstances of the man or woman who had asked for money.

An account of the work of the C.O.S. would be too long to give here. Suffice it to say that the activities which they started are all part of our Social Services to-day. They did a fine pioneering job with the minimum of cash, and the maximum of hard work, devotion and skill. I am always glad that I worked in their Baker Street office. They taught me an incalculable amount, and I found the case histories of the people they were helping very interesting; I learnt about the machinery of Local Government, also how to get on with other people in the office in which one worked.

I think there may have been one typewriter in the Baker Street office—certainly not more. Most of the letters were done by hand, and all the staff were volunteers. It was a cheerful place, and there were a great many jokes repeated and smiled at in any lull in the work. It was a drab, shabby little house, but there was a constructive and happy spirit there. I recall an incident which caused amusement. It was suggested that I should be sent to visit a family to ask some question about a job they wished to do. An argument arose in the office about whether I was fit to go to the especially slummy area in which this family lived. I was eager to see it for myself and went off, only to discover that one of the men in the office had followed me and stationed himself in the street outside the house where I was asking a few questions. This had a comic sequel when one of the men of the poor family meeting the C.O.S. worker, said indignantly, "I know Miss Grosvenor very well. I sweep the crossing in Grosvenor Square."

It was true, and he and I had been friends for some years. Later I sent him an invitation to my wedding, to which he came.

I left the C.O.S. office when I married, but continued doing work on juvenile employment. This mostly consisted in interviewing parents and trying to help them in the difficult matter of apprenticing their boys to a trade where, although their son might start with lower wages than he would get if he went into a "blind alley" job (such as selling newspapers at street corners), he would be steadily employed.

It is slightly amusing in these days of endless form-filling, and enquiries by Government officials into all that we do, to remember how strongly the recipients of the C.O.S. help objected to even the mildest and most tactful questioning about their family circumstances. People were far more individualistic in those days, and disliked having their private affairs discussed even when they had asked for help.

A prominent member of the C.O.S., Herbert Woollcombe, one of the most charming people I have ever known, a man to whose foresight and intelligence this country owes much, told me that he was once asked to give a lecture on Tennyson. When the talk was over, his chairman called for questions. A man stood up in the audience and said that he didn't care twopence about Tennyson, but he did know that the Charity Organisation Society should be swept off the face of the earth.

My mother did not quite approve of my C.O.S. activities; she feared that dowdiness and welfare work might go hand in hand. This was strange, as she worked hard herself at a variety of good causes. However, I persevered in my apprenticeship to the C.O.S. I had no special artistic talent as she had, and I knew in my heart that hard work and an outside interest were what I most needed to help me through the difficult years of growing up. I was also deeply interested in the problems of poverty. The C.O.S. office in Baker Street gave me an insight into these problems which has helped me all the rest of my life.

I went not long ago to speak at a meeting with several people of academic distinction at an educational establishment. As we mounted the platform, I said to a member of the committee, "I feel rather odd here because I never had any proper education," to which she replied strangely, though very kindly, "That's why we like you so much."

I wondered as I sat down on my narrow chair on the speakers' dais and listened to the educationalists talking, just what value I had gained from that very odd and patchy series of experiments that were called my education. If the kindly lady who said I was liked meant it seriously, perhaps I had received something that had its value?

My sister and I had a governess of whom we were very fond; she was nice-looking and very neatly dressed. We wasted a great deal of our time trying to find out her age. We laid every conceivable trap for her, but she was too much for us, and until she was quite an old woman (years after she had left us), we never discovered her age at all.

Unfortunately for us, she had absolutely no teaching ability at all. I was always puzzled by the fact that subjects which interested me keenly outside the schoolroom fell dead from dullness the moment we started our lessons. Our governess's moral standards were very high, and my mother, when I reproached her (after I was grown up) for not having got us a better teacher, replied that she always felt that moral standards were the most important thing of all.

Well, in a way she was right. If in these days of lower standards of honesty I am ever tempted to stray off the straight and narrow path of integrity, I am pulled up at once by remembering how horrified my dear old governess would have been. But we learnt little else from her. I progressed somewhat in history and in English subjects, from having a natural bent that way, but my arithmetic was non-existent, and in fact I never knew what the whole thing was about. My geography was deplorable. John, who could with ease hold the geography of a country in his head, used to laugh at me when we travelled abroad. He was wont to say that I would never be surprised if I suddenly encountered Constantinople in the middle of France, so nebulous were my ideas of where places were situated. My mother sent me to good classes when I was in London, and saw to it that I learnt drawing and studied languages and French, German and Italian literature; but it was all unrelated and unco-ordinated.

Looking back, it seems to me that few people then grasped the importance of good teaching. It is not understood even now as it should be, and people are allowed to teach who have not the faintest gift for it.

The conversation of clever people who came to our house and the houses of other members of our family was considered good for us. We certainly heard a great deal that was very interesting in this way, and what I heard often comes back to me echoing over the years. It helped to form our minds.

We had no competition at all, but we were not alone in this.

Blanche Dugdale writes in her delightful autobiography, *Family Homespun*, "Perhaps the oddest thing about my upbringing was its utter lack of any experience in competition or in measuring my attainments with those of my contemporaries. It never occurred to me to wonder whether I was backward or forward, clever or stupid. Beyond Mamma's (Lady Frances Balfour) *ad hoc* exhortations to 'show a little intelligence' nobody ever applied such words to me either in praise or criticism. In this there was perhaps some loss, but certainly there was much gain. Remarkably little of my time was spent in thinking about myself, an abnormal amount in thinking of the people I lived with."

The only time when I myself competed was when we did lessons with Cicely (Mrs. Lambton) and Katharine Horner (Mrs. Raymond Asquith). At the furthest stretch of my faculties I carried off a history prize. I enjoyed this time very much.

My education was supplemented by endless reading, and later with my husband's help and guidance I progressed in historical study. I have worked hard for years at Adult Education for others, as I firmly believe that the education you get for yourself after you are grown up has a very special value. But I still mourn the fact that I was never taught to concentrate or to have exactness of mind when I was a child, and that I was never told of their vital importance in later life. Every child should be taught these two things, as it is exceedingly hard to learn concentration and exactness of mind when you have left childhood behind.

We drew profiles on our copy books and showed up sloppy and inaccurate work. We were scolded for this, but I don't think we were as much to blame as our elders, who should have seen that all was not well with our education.

SERVANTS

NO chronicle, however slight, of the days of my youth is complete without some account of the servants of those days; but I must again emphasise that I am only writing of what I saw myself, and I cannot pretend to have a first-hand knowledge of the lodging-house slavey, or the workhouse drudge.

But I can write what I remember of those who served in the larger houses, many of whom were my friends for countless years. Servants, in my childhood, came young to a large house, worked very hard, were promoted, worked less hard as the years went by; were caught up into an empyrean where they had a sitting-room of their own. They then wore a black silk dress and were waited on by the under-servants. When they got too old for work, they usually retired on a pension with perquisites of a substantial kind, or sometimes they stayed until their, or their employer's, death.

This throwing in of their lot with a family brought its own reward. They were the closest friends of the children from birth, and really, I think, came to regard all of them almost as their own. "Soey," my grandmother's maid, a mellow virgin, who, when I first remember her, had long attained the black silk stage, was my constant companion. It was my slightly shuddering delight to hear her talking to her friends, especially to Mrs. Blackistone, Aunt Lily's maid. Like two sombre ravens, their talk always ran on gloomy topics, and the seamy side of things. I remember sitting unobserved and trembling, while "Blackie" related to "Soey" a story which culminated in these words: "And he threw an orange at her, and he hit her there" (touching her ample bust), "and she died at once." I never discovered the name of the fragile and tragically fated "she," but the story haunted me for years. No one has written more brilliantly on the subject of servants of this kind than H. G. Wells in his account of the inmates of Bladesover Park in *Tono Bungay*. "Soey" and "Blackie" seemed to live again in his pages.

The children in a big house knew more about what went on there than the grown-ups. Remarks were often made in front of us which were meant to percolate to our elders, and often household rules were modified because of this. Sometimes people say now how easy life must have been when there were plenty of servants. Life certainly was more comfortable, but human relationships are never easy, and a housemaid, butler or cook had an unequalled power of taking it out of their master or mistress in subtle ways. Orders could be received with veiled sulks and insinuations of trouble in the background. To any sensitive person, this caused such a sinking of the heart, that all the pleasure of welcoming friends to their house completely fled.

I remember hearing in a house in Scotland that the elderly butler, long established as a tyrant, showed his displeasure with the younger members of the family by lightly pushing the hot rim of a dish which he was handing them at dinner, against their cheeks. This is a true story, if an unusual one.

I have read in a recent book, and indeed have often heard it said, that we householders of to-day are expiating the sins of our forebears, in the reluctance of any but a small number of people to seek employment in private houses. This statement, to my mind, shows a lack of clear thinking and of knowledge of the past. It should be discussed and probed, as it does so little justice to the servants themselves. They came, as the saying is, in all sorts, good, bad and indifferent; but, at their best, they were fine and responsible people, and experts at their different jobs. A table laid under the auspices of a butler, with shining plate and china, had style and beauty. The head housemaid knew everything about the care of beautiful and probably fragile linen, and was the guardian of valuable china, pictures, carpets and hangings. The cook was usually an artist, and, although she had certainly first-class materials for cooking ready to her hand, she also knew how to cook them. In a country house all the basic food came from the estate, and the fruit and vegetables were grown by gardeners who thoroughly knew their job.

The upper servants passed their own expertise on to the under servants. A village mother would take endless pains to get her girl into what was called "a good house," where she could get a thorough training in some branch of specialised domestic work; or she would try to get her daughter into a vicarage where perhaps two maids were kept and where the vicar's wife had high standards of order.

No one wants training like that nowadays. The trend is all away from the home, and even the government urges married women to go into factories. The female sex are showing a distaste for the domesticity into which they have been clamped down for so many centuries. Their eyes are wistfully fixed on the United States, where they believe that they could get every labour-saving gadget for a house that their hearts could desire. And why not? They have well deserved them for their patient labour through the centuries.

The master (and above all the mistress) of a house, of course, set the tone of it. If they were indifferent to their own comfort and that of their guests, the efficiency of the service in the house slackened and grew casual. One famous country house I knew well, was much criticised for the badness of its service. It was whispered that, when the host and hostess were at their shooting lodge in Scotland, they returned unexpectedly to find their butler comfortably ensconced in the drawing-room on a sofa, fast asleep.

One great difficulty in a big household (of which any conscientious mistress of a house was well aware) was that the older servants were inclined to overwork the younger ones. This was hard to prevent, and any remonstrances on an employer's part were apt to be met by the stony reply, "I did this when I was young. Why shouldn't she (or he) do it now?" It was almost impossible to make them move from this point of view. The youngest and latest-joined member of a household staff was apt to be treated as a dog's-body and to run hither and thither all day; but so, I should imagine, is the latest recruit in a factory or a hospital.

I should not, however, pretend for a moment that the work of the upper servants was light. They had to oversee the work of a house, and in the pre-bathroom days, cans of hot water were taken to the bedrooms of the family and the guests. Sometimes writers and others indulge in nostalgic remarks about the cosiness of sitting in a bath in front of a bedroom fire. But it was only cosy up to a point, as the can of water was apt to be too hot, and, when you had cooled it down by pouring in cold water, it rapidly became too chilly for comfort.

It is idle to blame one's forebears as they lived in a different mental climate from ours. But, if we *are* concerned to raise our eyebrows with wonder tinged with disapproval, it might be on the subject of their building activities. The Victorians loved bricks and mortar, and they not only built what is ugly by any standard, but they also had a positive genius for inconvenience in their own houses.

Often when someone inherited a graceful Georgian house with a staircase with shallow steps, wide landings and beautifully-shaped rooms, they would add a large wing which was not only out of keeping with the earlier house, but which contained the maximum amount of flights of steps, long passages, and in fact everything that was as un-labour-saving as possible. This made the work of the servants far harder than was necessary.

I have myself suffered acutely from the Victorian addition to our own house. The Parsons family purchased Elsfield Manor from the North family somewhere about the early eighteen-seventies. At that time it was a charming two-storied house. They proceeded to pull half of it down, and to build a tall addition to it leaving their unfortunate successors with a large basement and the steepest backstairs possible to imagine. I once talked to Miss Parsons about this when she was nearly ninety. She laughed happily, and remarked, "Well, we always said we had a very long-legged architect." I did not smile, but said grimly, "Well, that staircase is the bane of my existence."

Servants' bedrooms were not always comfortable, and were apt to be furnished with odd chairs and tables from other parts of the house: and undoubtedly behind the baize door there was not nearly enough care taken about renewing worn-out objects. But children also had bare nurseries furnished with left-overs from the rest of the house. I remember that our nursery at Moor Park was severely plain and shabby. We had no whimsical pictures on the walls of rabbits or squirrels, and no chairs and tables adapted to our smallness of stature. We knocked up against hard surfaces and uncompromising corners, thus being prepared for some of the harshnesses of adult life. The rooms of the just grown-up members of the family had faded chintzes and rickety chairs. No one expected anything different, and the cosy and reassuring creak of an elderly wicker chair I still remember with pleasure, when I sat talking to another girl of my ideas about life. Bedrooms were much used as bed-sitting-rooms, which seems odd in large houses with plenty of rooms to spare.

It would have been considered vulgar and *nouveau riche* to have a luxurious bedroom, even if such a thing had been possible in pre-central-heating days. Best bedrooms had good beds with fine linen and soft pillows. At the foot of the bed there would be a sofa, and beyond that a writing table, complete with an ornamented blotting book, and inkstand very often of ormolu or some pretty china.

The dressing-table, where the mirror was flanked with tall china candlesticks, was solidly built. There were plenty of drawers in the dressing-table and writing-table, and a fire would be lit about tea-time in the polished grate. There was plenty of room to put the various objects brought by visitors who made long visits. The Victorian bedroom had an uncramped feeling of space to move about in. I should like one myself now, and I should also like to recapture the sense of peace and leisure that I once knew. I can imagine how delightful it would be to sit there quietly writing. But, on the whole, I would say that the comfort of houses in the late Victorian era has been greatly exaggerated, by those who have no idea of how people lived in those days.

To begin with, the houses were very cold. The passages struck an icy chill. When children were recovering from colds, they were enveloped in shawls when they went down to the drawing-room. In fact, they resembled Eskimos equipped for the rigours of an Arctic winter. It is true that fires glowed comfortably enough in sitting-rooms, but the moment you were outside the orbit of the fire, draughts played all round you, and your feet became as cold as stones.

Some people were fresh-air maniacs. They flung open every window, and the epithet "stuffy" was often on their lips. These fresh-air fiends were usually sportsmen who had spent long hours in the open air, or ladies who had been out hunting, walking or gardening. On the whole, most people sat as near to the chimney-piece as they could, and men who enjoyed standing with their backs to the fire, holding forth about politics or agriculture to the assembled company, thus blocking heat from coming into the room, were more tolerated than loved. The inhabitants of country houses suffered from endless colds and chilblains, and I was amused to find, in looking through my family letters, how much time the writers spent in telling each other about the progress of their colds and chills. Illness was looked upon differently from nowadays; it was like a saga which went on and on through the years. Now, the majority of people have an operation or a "cure," and start again, though certain diseases like rheumatism seem to continue, and to be as incurable as ever.

Most people would not now take kindly to the slower tempo of life of the pre-machine age. There was so much time when nothing happened, which would be unendurable to people of a later age. I remember reading of a girl in the eighteenth century whose father suffered so much from *ennui* in his country house, that she surreptitiously put saffron into his tea. This was then considered a sovereign cure for depression and gloom. In a quiet country life there were days of even routine and of extreme peace. This had its good and its bad sides; it led to the magnifying of trifles, and to an intensely personal attitude to life. People quarrelled easily, became heated by little things, foibles were magnified, and the machinery of a house which could work so well and harmoniously, jarred and creaked; men and women, instead of trying to improve their characters, often cherished their failings.

"You know Aunt A. doesn't like this or that," "Uncle B. won't put up with the other," and so on. This petulance and giving way to feelings existed alongside of great patience and sweetness, and there was usually one member of the family who spent her life in smoothing over servants and relatives, and trying to make everything as pleasant as possible. No wonder she looked a trifle haggard and careworn.

This mode of life made for a tight and idiosyncratic family life, and led all the members of a family to take a deep interest in each other. Families were a little like tribes, and to enter into the house of one of these clans was formidable to the young and shy. Speaking for myself, I feel that we have lost a great deal. There are few meeting-places now for families; entertaining is much restricted, and there is a thinning out of social contacts. You cannot have omelettes without breaking eggs, and two wars are considerable omelettes, which have smashed the life I am trying to describe. But I have twice visited Paris since the war, and have come away each time with a pang of envy at the amount of social life which the French have still managed to preserve.

I have spoken so much about the country that I feel I must also write briefly about the London of my childhood. When I was a smallish child, I was taken by older members of my family to some of the larger London houses. They had something of the atmosphere of the country in them. Before the days of machine-driven traffic, the noise of London was muffled and sleepy, with the clop, clop of horses' feet and the chattering of sparrows audible in the silence. The owners of these large houses appeared, to my eyes, to be living in much the same way as they did on their country estates. They walked and drove along streets, or in Hyde Park, instead of country lanes, at the same hours of the day. They attended Court functions and went to balls in other large houses, and usually took an interest in some form of charity. In the few months that she was in London each year, my grandmother worked so faithfully in helping the Sick Children's Hospital in Great Ormond Street, that they named a ward the Ebury Ward in her memory.

London smelt of dust, and water-carts sprayed it. I can recall the pleasant, damp smell which arose in Hyde Park when this had just been done. Hansoms went slowly or rapidly along, jingling as they did so. It was always exciting to look and see if you could glimpse a girl with her mamma, or a young man whom you happened to know, sitting by himself. Few vehicles devised by man can have been more uncomfortable or more dangerous than a hansom. It seems incredible now that I ever climbed into one, dressed in an ample-skirted party dress which someone tried to shield from contact with a mud-coated wheel. When I did manage to get up the step and settle myself inside, my large flower-trimmed hat took up most of the space in the little compartment. It is laughable to think how easily we all now insert ourselves into low, streamlined cars, wearing small hats and shortened skirts.

I recall that my aunt, Mary Lovelace, when the existence of motor cars was finally forced upon her attention, consented reluctantly to go for a drive in one of the new-fangled monsters. It was low and narrow in shape, and she hit her head as she got into it. The small section of landscape she could see out of the window struck her as meagre and unsatisfactory.

"Made for weasels, dear, made for weasels," she was heard to murmur to herself.

When my mother and I were driving in a hansom we often saw streets and squares through a dazzle of raindrops, when the glass was lowered in front of us to the level on which it met the folding panel of wood, which covered the passengers' legs from rain and mud. I regret the hansoms in a way; they were so utterly absurd and unpractical. When they and four-wheelers vanished off the streets, a comic, grotesque element went away for ever. Taxi-drivers in the blitz in London were both funny and heroic, and Cockney wit still flourishes, but the traffic, to look at, is just as standardised as in any other western capital.

PART III

Portrait of a House

This was Moor Park, when I was acquainted with it, and the sweetest place, I think, that I have been in my life, either before or since, at home or abroad; what it is now I can give little account, having passed through several hands that have made great changes in the gardens as well as houses; but the remembrance of what it was is too pleasant ever to forget, and therefore I do not believe to have mistaken the figure of it, which may serve for a pattern to the best gardens of our manner, and that are most proper for our country and climate.

SIR WILLIAM TEMPLE.

HISTORICAL BACKGROUND

MOOR PARK, which now lies between Northwood and Rickmansworth, began as marsh and river-bed. The property was named by the harmonious title of Manor of the Moor, and was bestowed on the Monastery of St. Albans by Offa, King of Mercia. We know that the monks made fishponds, but nothing else has survived to their memory.

Moor Park remained in the hands of the Church, passing from the monks, who were presumably vowed to poverty, into the hands of no less a person than George Nevil, brother of Warwick the Kingmaker. This splendid prelate liked to do things in the grand manner. He enclosed six hundred acres of land from his park in 1460 and built himself a palace which has long since disappeared, leaving no trace of even its foundations.

Archbishop Nevil fell with dramatic suddenness. After he had been granted the Manor by Edward IV he grew steadily in wealth and power, a dangerous matter in those days. In 1471 the Archbishop invited the king, fresh from his exile in Flanders, to a great feast. The preparations for the feast were finished, the sumptuous gold plate laid out upon the table, when retribution fell swift and sure in the shape of a summons from Windsor on a charge of high treason, followed by imprisonment and disgrace.

We next hear of Moor Park forty odd years afterwards, when it fell to Cardinal Wolsey as one of the prizes of his rising fortunes. Wolsey's red leather-covered saddle stood always in one corner of the hall, in my childhood. It is probable that the wise Cardinal spent a good deal of time at Moor Park. There is a legend that under the oak tree near the Northwood lodge, called Cardinal Wolsey's oak, he used to sit and meditate. Legend also tells that Henry VIII met his sharp-eyed, black-browed lady love, Anne Boleyn, more than once under the Cardinal's roof. Cardinal Wolsey fell from power in 1529, and again there is silence about Moor Park.

In 1547 it must have been splendidly furnished, as we are told that an inventory was made of thirty-nine pages, giving a list of 125 tapestries, carpets, beds, also furniture of other kinds of great richness.

In 1577 Queen Elizabeth granted Moor Park to Francis Russell, second Earl of Bedford. It continued in the Russell family till 1613, when it reverted to the Crown, and was granted by James I in 1617 absolutely to Edward, the third Earl of Bedford. His wife Lucy constructed the gardens, which were so beautiful that no one could speak of them without extravagance. In 1626 she sold it to William, third Earl of Pembroke; he was succeeded by Philip, fourth Earl, who sold it in 1631 to Robert, Earl of Monmouth. Henry, Earl of Monmouth, sold Moor Park in 1652 to Sir Richard Franklyn, who lived there eleven years and then sold it to James Butler, first Duke of Ormonde. Shortly after Ormonde's death it was sold in 1670 to the unhappy Duke of Monmouth, natural son of Charles II. Monmouth joined in the Rye House plot, for which offence he was banished from Court, and retired to Moor Park. After Charles's death in 1685 Monmouth conspired against James II, and raised the flag of rebellion. Defeated at the battle of Sedgemoor, he was tried for high treason and beheaded on Tower Hill at the age of thirty-six. James granted the estates of Moor Park to Monmouth's widow, Anne, Duchess of Monmouth and Buccleuch, who married secondly in 1688 the third Lord Cornwallis.

Henry VIII and Anne Boleyn were not the only famous lovers who stayed at Moor Park. Sir William Temple walked in the gardens and composed letters to his charming Dorothy Osborne, whose home was Chicksands Priory. She was a cousin of the Franklyns who were then living at Moor Park. It would appear that she was not on good terms with them, for though she in her turn wrote to Sir William Temple about Moor Park, she says little or nothing about the house and much about the gardens. When, however, Dorothy and Sir William were married they spent their honeymoon at Moor Park in 1655, and so great was the spell it cast upon them, that they named their own house in Surrey, Moor Park.

Moor Park—the Front of the House

Moor Park—the Gardens

Moor Park—Marble Doorway

To return to the owners of Moor Park, Anne, Duchess of Monmouth, sold the property in 1720 to Mr. Benjamin Styles, whose fortune came from that early but magnificent excursion in company-promoting, the South Sea Company. Styles was brother-in-law to Sir John Eyles, sub-governor of the South Sea Company; he therefore possessed inside knowledge of how matters stood, and sold out before the Bubble burst.

Benjamin Styles turned his attention to the alteration of the house. When he purchased Moor Park, it was generally conjectured that the house which Monmouth had built about 1670 was one of the best pieces of brickwork in England. With a lack of veneration for the past, which makes us shudder, Styles determined to spend a fortune in turning a Stuart house into a Palladian palace. He may have suffered from *la folie de grandeur*, but he certainly summoned the best available talent to his aid. Monmouth's building was recased in Portland stone, and Sir James Thornhill, the fashionable painter of ceilings, was put in charge of the interior decorations. Several Italian artists, Leoni, Amiconi, and others, worked at the painting, while Thornhill painted the saloon and the hall himself.

Styles quarrelled with Thornhill when the bill for all the decorations came to be due. He declared himself dissatisfied with the work, although Thornhill had only charged him the comparatively modest sum of £3,500. Styles took the matter into court, and the case was decided against him. He was made to pay Thornhill an extra £500. Thornhill was unlucky in his dealing with anyone connected with the South Sea Company. The directors of the Company refused to pay him more than twenty-five shillings a yard for their hall, which he had filled with paintings of gods and goddesses. That, they said, was his price for the Blenheim decorations, and no more would they pay.

Styles spent £150,000 on Moor Park, and his successor in 1754, Lord Anson, the victor of the battle of Cape Finisterre, a large sum on the garden. Lord Anson brought in Capability Brown, who planned the garden and pleasure grounds, so entirely worthy of their name. Horace Walpole, that acute observer of weak points, says in 1766, however, "Nothing is done to the house.

There are not even chairs in the great apartment." On the other hand, it is said that Lord Anson brought to Moor Park the Chinese paper in the "Blue Room" as a trophy, after a voyage round the world.

Doctor Johnson visited Lord Anson and wrote a stately poem on the Temple of the Winds in the pleasure ground.

Each successive owner of Moor Park went on beautifying and adding to it. Lord Anson's brother, Thomas Anson, sold the estate to Sir Laurence Dundas, a successful army contractor, and the founder of the Zetland family. Cipriani decorated the dining-room for him, and he brought the Dancing Hours chimneypiece from a Borghese palace. In 1785 Thomas Bates Rous pulled down the wings, which contained a chapel as well as domestic offices.

Lord Westminster[1] altered the gardens and park, when he bought the place in 1808 without ever seeing it. He put up the Chinese paper in the dining-room. Later on our grandfather[2] went down to Moor Park with his father. They rode together from London, and Grandpapa only commented in his diary that "We thought the windows seemed very narrow," which argues a high standard in this matter!

The "Green Drive" round the park was made by Lord Westminster when King William IV and Queen Adelaide came to Moor Park.

I have written down the history of Moor Park, houses, gardens, and lands—a chess-board on which have moved and been check-mated, Kings, Queens, Bishops, and pawns. Moor Park has seen many generations of people, all of whom loved its beauty and who tried to leave some mark upon house or lands. There is an elusive quality about the place. It has never allowed itself to be the possession of any family for very long. Our family lived there just under a hundred years, but it has left us with an abiding memory of beauty and grace.

[1] 1st Marquis of Westminster.

[2] Robert Grosvenor, created 1st Lord Ebury.

2

MOOR PARK. EARLY RECOLLECTIONS

M Y earliest recollections of Moor Park are of great spaces
with winds blowing across them, endless playgrounds, and
a house so lofty that it reached almost to the sky. It contained
innumerable passages, made for wet-day explorations, and an
infinity of rooms. My memory reaches back to the time when
I was about three years old, when the furniture towered above
me, and I thought that my mother was suspended between heaven
and earth, as I burrowed in the woolly rug by the side of her bed.

The central figures of a child's hierarchy are its parents, but
my grandmother came very close to them. After that there was
a long gap, and Soey, her ancient maid, and my uncles and aunts,
stood more or less on the same level, though my American aunt
was on a pinnacle of her own.

My father's elder brother, Thomas Grosvenor, when he was
a young attaché in Pekin married Sophie Wells Williams, the
daughter of the United States Minister there. She had been
brought up in China and was a woman of beauty, intelligence
and charm.

One of my earlier recollections is of sitting by the fire in her
bedroom at Moor Park while she popped corn for us on an
instrument poked between the bars of the grate. This resembled
a small wire cage at the end of a long stick which she held in
her hand. She told us stories of her Chinese childhood when
we were small children, and later on, as we grew older, of her
arrival at Moor Park. It must have been a terrifying ordeal. It
began by Uncle Tommy taking her to see my grandfather's old
keeper Ben Green, who eyed her doubtfully and said he hoped
she would make Mr. Thomas a respectable wife.

The first morning at Moor Park Aunt Sophie did not know
what to wear, and her husband, with manly lack of knowledge,
begged her to put on "something nice." She donned a rich black
silk dress which she had worn for a Court mourning at The Hague

and went down to the ordeal of family prayers, feeling doubtful and unhappy. After prayers she stood beside a table in the hall not knowing what to do next. My father's elder sister came up to her and asked her not to stand about looking "silk gownified." Aunt Sophie always added, "I could cheerfully have killed her."

Happily her never-failing sense of humour prevailed, and she explained to her new sister-in-law that all she knew of her husband's country was derived from Jane Austen's and Miss Braddon's books, but that neither of them had shed any light on what to wear on a sunny October morning in an English country house.

Life at Moor Park must have been confusing, to say the least of it, for a girl of New England, but Aunt Sophie was adaptable in character and although she could complain incisively about things in general, when she had done so she forgot her grievance and went on as before. She missed nothing of the scene around her, and viewed with temperate amusement the different shades of religious observance in her family-in-law, also their political opinions.

My grandmother regarded her new daughter-in-law with alarm, and at first held back from any intimacy with her, but she soon realised that someone from such a different background to herself could still be an admirable wife to her son and a charming companion to herself.

Uncle Tommy and Aunt Sophie did not, I imagine, come much to Moor Park during their married life, but after he died of pneumonia in St. Petersburg, my grandparents offered her a home, and she lived with them in London and at Moor Park till their death.

She had a vast bedroom at Moor Park which she also used as a sitting-room, and, as my uncle died before I was born, I can remember running in and out there from my earliest childhood. When I grew older I remember Aunt Sophie trying to teach me to put tiny stitches in the hems of handkerchiefs, with not a great deal of success, I fear. "Susan Charlotte, that's an *ass* of a way of doing things." I can still hear the exasperation in her voice as she vehemently pronounced "ass" to rhyme with "mass."

Moor Park. Early Recollections

My mother and I describe my grandmother[1] from different points of view, but with the same devout admiration. There can rarely have been any member of a large family who was so much beloved. She was very small and bent, and walked with a stick. A big bonnet framed soft grey curls and a beautifully defined face. Niece of the great Duke of Wellington, her aquiline nose recalled his famous one, without emulating it in size and angularity. Her blue eyes, clear and candid as a child's, looked you straight in the face. She often carried little devotional books in her hands, or her Church Service, a well-worn black book with limp covers now in my possession. She wore a gold watch-chain with onyxes at intervals, on which hung an intricate collection of seals. I used to turn them over and look at them while I sat on her knee. Her headgear in the house was a big cap with purple ribbons. Her austere black clothes were fashioned for hard and long wear, for all her spare money went secretly to the poor. Her whole life was unobtrusively lived for others, and was illumined by a religion which glowed through her daily actions like sunshine through a fine stained-glass window. My father was her most beloved child, and she was always specially tender to me. My life at Moor Park was lived a great deal in her room, which, having a curtain across it, she used for the double purpose of bedroom and sitting-room. An ardent homeopathist, she dosed me, when my mother permitted, with enormous sugar-coated pills and innocuous medicines, whose sweet and rather cloying taste I can still recall.

Her goodness to children was amazing. She would give me Bible lessons, read to me, talk to and play with me, as if she had no other thought or occupation in the world. I think she had a kind of freshness of mind which made her happy in the company of children. I was unshakably convinced that she was far younger than her own daughters, her attitude towards youthful indiscretions being so much less rigid and Olympian than theirs. They certainly took life more solemnly than she did. Children have queer touchstones of their own for youth and age.

We always started the week-days at Moor Park with prayers.

[1] *Née* Charlotte Arbuthnot Wellesley, daughter of 1st Lord Cowley.

A preliminary gong was rung, making a formidable sound, difficult to ignore, as it reverberated through the big house, always
ending in four strokes dealt harder than the rest, which sounded
almost savage in their intensity. Everyone down to the youngest
kitchenmaid came trooping into the great hall. Generally a few
hasty footsteps were painfully audible from the gallery which
ran round the top of the hall, as some laggard looked over with
guilty haste, to see if he or she could be in their place in time;
no easy matter with long passages to be traversed, and a long
flight of steps to run down. The servants were lined up opposite
the family and guests—an arrangement pleasing to my childish
soul, as it always gave me something of human interest to look at.

Prayers were short and simple. I remember a strong feeling
of annoyance at Auntie B., who always seemed to know every
psalm by heart; while I laboured slowly, battling with the written
word and always behindhand, for the pace set by our elders was
too rapid for my years. As I write, recollections come sweeping
over me of kneeling with my face pressed against the sympathetic
surface of the rubbed and faded scarlet leather, covering the tops
of the long stools with their gold twisted carvings, while wafts
of warm stale air came up through gratings from the antique
steam-heating system.

It is amazing what a number of impressions, speculations and
surmises a child can receive and formulate during a short space
of time. My thoughts used to fly far and wide, seeking solution
of such problems as "What made Mrs. Robson's (the cook) nose
so red?" "What would the other children choose to play at?"
With a passing wonder at the melancholy ferocity of the Psalms
of David.

The hall made a noble background to thought, as it soared
above me to culminate in the painted ceiling. Racks with hats
and coats, old and new, stood at one end, and marble tables at
the other. In the middle was a wide space of marble floor. On
one side stood a huge writing-table covered with a jumble of
books and writing materials. This has since been discovered to
be a very fine piece of Chippendale, by a generation which unites
the powers of Oscar Wilde's cynic and sentimentalist, and knows

not only the value but the price of everything. On the other side, a billiard-table with a faded cloth stood four-square to the world. On one of the marble tables was a clock which chimed, with musical precision, the quarter-hours of our lives. On each side of it crouched lions in brown alabaster, or, as I fancied, frozen jelly. I loved all these things, dimly realising their beauty. My fondest admiration was for the Chinese pagodas which stood on stands in two corners of the hall in tapering glass cases. They held for me all the mystery of the East. The little gilt bells seemed always to be summoning minute invisible worshippers to shadowy ceremonies inside white walls, which might have been made from sea foam or the fabric of dreams.

After prayers came breakfast. We had already partaken of ours, but were allowed to play with our toys while our elders fed. The dining-room, which ran the whole length of one side of the house, was, on a summer morning, a marvel of light and sunshine, with great French windows opening on to a broad balcony, where green vistas sloped and undulated to soft blue hills. There were various very beautiful things in the room. The old Chinese paper added an extra horizon to that given by its size. The "Dancing Hours" surmounted the marble mantelpiece, graceful white figures against a jewelled background of lapis-lazuli. There was a mellow leather screen, where gentlemen with cocked hats for ever caracoled and showed off on spirited steeds. It must have been a French one, as *Le Manège* was written underneath, to my fatal confusion of mind. At the beginning of my studies in that language I always read *manège* as *ménage*, and was accordingly puzzled.

I was fondest, I think, of the Aubusson carpet. It had a faded garland of roses at one end, near the windows overlooking the valley. Morning after morning I set my Noah's Ark animals round it in a ring—no easy task, as the quadrupeds had, by many breakages, become bipeds, and refused to defy the laws of gravitation by remaining upright. Through all our play we heard the news of the day discussed and commented on by the family party surrounding the big table in the middle of the room, with remarks on the lateness of my uncles for breakfast, and talk on all sorts of matters. Scraps of it half heard and half understood come back unbidden into my head even now. In the winter we played much the same games, but ran continually to the window to look at the fairy landscape and throw out crumbs to the hungry multitude of birds, whose regular *table d'hôte* it was during the cold months.

The ritual of the year is beloved by children, from the finding of the first snowdrops to the getting of holly for Christmas decorations, with long tracts of time between spring and summer, rich with flowers and scents, and the always newly thrilling episode of autumn fruits. A large part of our time was spent in the formal Italian garden. You ran down a flight of grey stone steps from the great saloon to paths between box-bordered beds. A low lichen-covered wall with big stone urns, filled with geraniums, divided it from the park. A fountain splashed musically, and goldfish gleamed in the water. A regrettable incident occurred, I remember, when my grandparents were visited by the great of the earth—the German Prince and Princess Radziwill. After having disgustedly realised that they were without the insignia of royalty so familiar to us in fairy stories, and after a solemn walk in which we paired off like the animals in the ark, and went in procession round the park and kitchen garden, Alice[1] and I retired into private life, had our tea and forgot our existence as units in the social world. In old clothes, grubby and dishevelled, we were next seen pursuing a tortoiseshell cat by leaps and bounds over the box-rimmed beds. We were summoned to the princely party, who were having tea on the terrace at the top of the steps, and our parents' feelings as we drew near, may be better imagined than described.

The Italian garden was bounded by a low wall. To the left lay the beautiful cultivated "wilderness," which sloped down to the broad terrace overlooking a little vale in the park. It was most artfully planned, with a cool fountain and big cedars, and clumps of flowering trees, and great bushes of azaleas, which

[1] Alice Grosvenor. See page 42.

radiated colour and light on hot days. A statue of Neptune, brown with age, with a pitcher in his hand from which water trickled, sat comfortably gazing in front of him, half-engulfed by a Portugal laurel, the embraces of which became more urgent as time went on. On my last visit to Moor Park about the year 1920, I parted the branches and looked at him as he sat entirely hidden. My grown-up years rolled away for a moment as I gazed down at the basin full of brown water, stiff dead laurel leaves, and wriggling tadpoles. It was the same as ever.

The broad terrace with a crumbling grey lichen-covered seat (William and Mary in date) at each end, looked over a tiny valley, and away beyond to a long vista of trees and blue distances. Moor Park had the most magnificent trees, especially oaks, which, leafy and majestic, stood like the memorials of an older age. Legend says that when it belonged at one time to the Duchess of Monmouth, she decapitated all the trees when her husband was beheaded, not, it is believed, from a grim and rather misplaced sense of humour, but from a wish to make them less valuable to the Government as timber. This may account for the squat solidity of some of their trunks.

All around and outside lay the park, to us our whole world, and a world of wonder and beauty. Will my reader imagine that we are going for a walk through the park together? We will go in from the Northwood lodge under an archway of stone. A child would want to linger on the right side of the road where it falls steeply down to a slope, covered with bracken, because there are such multitudes of rabbits running in and out, but older people will want to go up through the bracken to the left to where the famous Bath Clump towers above us. Then I think we will take my favourite path, a grass track leading from the lodge round the back of the Clump. We will imagine that it is evening and that the oaks are throwing long shadows on to the sunlit grass. I once found a hedgehog rooting there; he looked at me for a second with terror in his little eyes, and then cantered away. We then go down past the pleasure ground through the trees till we see the deer walking or lying on the grass, swishing their tails and looking up at us with a kind of nervous confidence.

When we get near to them they move away with quiet dignity.

The grey stones of the house show through the green leaves; and as we emerge, just a little above it, it lies solid, spacious and welcoming in its garden. It stands in a valley, or rather on a sort of shelf, as the ground beyond falls away steeply again towards Rickmansworth. On that side we could run headlong down into what always seemed to us another country. There was a farm, and a very nice stile, and watercress beds, and an old tree on which mistletoe grew. But we must walk back through the trees and up to the pleasure ground. It lay on the slope of the hill between the Northwood gate and the house. When I ran up the hill in childhood, it was steep enough to make me hot and panting; I had not then attained to those years, so-called, of discretion, when you go up hills in a manner more economical of your strength. I opened a grille, ascended two short flights of steps by the side of which cool and unruffled stone Cupids smiled down on me. I usually paused on the soft green turf at the top, and stared at a moss-grown statue under a cedar tree, a seat green with age, and a rush-rimmed pond. In June this pond was encircled by rhododendrons whose reflections in the water might have rivalled the necklace of Prester John in colour and brilliance. Opposite the statue, cedar, and seat, on the other side of the pond, rose another slope crowned by trees under whose shade was a temple in stone and stucco, giving the whole scene that touch of Nature assisted by art, so characteristic of the eighteenth century.

This pleasure ground was the scene of all our happiest games, and the centre of our thoughts and dreams. As a child I gathered acorns and blackberries, and earliest snowdrops there, and when I was older dreamed away golden afternoons under the cedar, when there was no sound except the occasional fall of a leaf into the quiet water. The pond froze in anything like a hard winter, and all and sundry gathered to skate. I remember often seeing Uncle Algy, a beautiful skater, doing figures and waltzing on the ice, while we children pounded round and round in more pedestrian enjoyment.

The kitchen gardens lay at the top of the other slope which

overlooked the park, on the left of the road as you walked
through from Northwood to Rickmansworth. We walked delicately here (like Agag), flying before Mundell, a sinister figure
like most gardeners, and the sworn enemy of children.

I have no space to enlarge on the milk house, cool and damp,
with the blue and white china on the table. In the middle of it
stood a brown china bull, easily the most beautiful thing in the
world to my youthful mind. Or the farm, with its tiny duck-
pond in front, just like a child's drawing. Yet all these were contained in the magic circle of the park. Beyond, on the other side
of the road, we peeped at picturesque cottages with box bushes
in front of them.

I left my picture of the house abruptly, after describing breakfast. Luncheon came heralded by the gong. I remember Auntie
Siss[1] bringing her knitting and trying to silence any fidgety child
by tapping her with inordinately long knitting-needles. My uncles
at every meal buried their milky puddings under sugar with a
generosity that any food-controller of to-day would shiver to
think of. The fruit was always wonderful, coming from the high
sun-warmed walls of the kitchen garden. The nectarines were,
especially, things to remember; also the famous Moor Park apri-
cots. A particularly translucent golden jam was made from them
in which a white almond floated. I remember in *Mansfield Park*
how Mrs. Norris speaks of an apricot tree in her garden being
a very fine one, "in fact a real Moor Park."

Tea came, set in the saloon. You walked from the dining-
room through a little square chamber into this long drawing-
room. I have said nothing of the decoration of Moor Park, which
was of a bold and florid kind. Above the lovely *boiseries* with
faint gold ornamentation, the staircase, saloon and hall were
painted with life-size figures of Io and the Bull, Pluto and
Proserpine. A party of women from the East End of London
were brought down for the day, and one of them was heard
to comment admiringly upon "them lovely 'oly pictures." They

[1] My father's sister, Victoria Grosvenor.

somehow fitted into the whole grandiose conception of the house, and certainly added to its sense of size and space. The whole family sat round tables laden with good things produced from the still-room. (The little tiny buns made there, and the jams, oh, how good they were!) There were big white cups with pink rims to them, out of which the family drank weak tea, known as "Grosvenor wash." In the summer, sunlight and scents of hay and heliotrope drifted in from the Italian garden; in the winter, fires blazed and lamps with fluted paper shades stood comfortably about on tables. Beyond the saloon was the Blue Room, whose jewel-like Chinese paper made it seem less like a room than a fairy garden, revealing infinite vistas of queer forests. The White Room beyond it again had white pillars at one end and a lovely ceiling. Its chief charm to us children lay in its outlook towards our goal in life, the pleasure ground. Jessamine grew on the steps leading down to the garden, and a pleasanter room could not be imagined. Beyond it was a little passage, a fine library, and then you had completed the circle and were back in the hall.

My grandfather, erect and very slight, always wore black clothes with a high collar. He was very kind to the troop of grandchildren who played about his house. His interests were those of a country gentleman—but of one who had always played a part in public affairs. He was much concerned with matters of ritual, and carried on long correspondences about church problems. There is a legend that he wrote a charmingly affectionate note to Lady B. of B. before her marriage, and at the same time one to a certain Dean about the Athanasian creed, and then put them into the wrong envelopes, adding perhaps a further touch of confusion to that already difficult subject.

A child's memory is a curious thing. It partakes of the Bergsonian doctrine of duration. In my recollections time flowed evenly on with the curious phenomenon that people were always doing the same things. Auntie Siss, for instance, cannot always have been playing a piano or organ, or driving about in a carriage drawn by ponies. Yet when I remember Auntie Siss I see nothing but vivid pictures of her doing these two things, through tracts and aeons of time. She and Auntie B. were a curious contrast physically. Auntie Siss was not only tall but very massive, unlike the rest of the family, who were tall but spare of flesh. She had a very high courage, as her size must have made everything laborious. An admirable whip, her ponies and cart were a feature of the countryside. The cart rocked to its foundations when she got in or out of it, but that made no difference to her work at Rickmansworth, her conduct of choir practices, or her playing of the organ in church. She disarmed ridicule by gaily leading the laugh against herself. "When I've said I'm fat there's really nothing more to be said," she remarked to her nieces one day, and it was true.

Of Auntie B. there was very little body and much spirit. Her lips moved as if she was praying continually. Her life of good work and almost conventual self-discipline should have been as a city set on a hill of example to the younger generation. We loved—and feared—both her and Auntie Siss, as their righteous wrath occasionally, and most deservedly, came down upon us; but, looking back, I feel how long-suffering they were and how strangely little severe. Both ardently religious, they were only dissuaded, when my grandfather died, by the united efforts of the family, from going respectively to Japan and Assyria as missionaries. Auntie B.'s fragile health and extreme lameness, and Auntie Siss's unwieldiness, apart from anything else, made it impossible. Instead, they settled down to a life of good works, kindness, and religious observances, in a little house in Cheyne Walk, and died, one in 1913, and the other in 1914.

The mode of life at Moor Park was somewhat unusual even in those days. People have told me that it reminded them of a French *ménage* when the whole family lives together. It was fraught with difficulties and endless possibilities of friction to the older generation, but to us children it was Paradise. It meant having all our cousins to play with, and we played hard and continuously. Alice and I were inseparable. In a fit of what must have been cannibalistic frenzy I once bit her arm in the stuffy gloom behind a clothes basket in the passage, during a game of hide and seek; but after that singular episode I never remember quarrelling with her again. But our scrapes were legion. I could go on filling books about Moor Park, but I haven't done so, and in rereading this sketch I realise that I haven't told half that I should like to tell. But I fear that by piling up details I should only obscure vision and not clarify it. I have loved Moor Park all my life with such tenacity that spiritually it is still mine though others possess it. It has made a background and a setting to so many pictures in my brain, and fixed my tastes and standards irrevocably. To this day I can't smell heliotrope, lilac, or hay, without being a child there again, and some day if I am rich I shall hire a mowing machine to mow each May morning outside my window when I wake. I shall feel, perhaps, that I am still lying behind the curtain which cut off a section of our enormous nursery (it was brown with yellow spots and always reminded me of the top of an omelette). On all sides were windows, open, from one of which we saw into the heart of a cedar tree, whose groups of cones standing in the branches were like dull people at a garden party. I fear that Heaven is the only place where I shall have the same soaring awakening of the spirit, the same sense of infinite possibility again, and perhaps some friendly angel will mow grass for me, while I lie and plan what I shall do all day with the zest and fervency of a child.

I end with two quotations. My mother wrote about the changes at Moor Park: "It is now a golf club and the park has rows of villas which make it unrecognisable. Luckily I do not have to see these changes, and I still believe that were I to wander up the drive from Rickmansworth or down from the Batchworth Heath Lodge, I should find everything as I left it, perhaps a little dustier, a little more faded, and with ghosts for inhabitants. But if, as time goes on, I am forced to realise the changed aspect of things, I still have my memories, the terrace on a night in June, with the great house behind us humming with life, the wide canopy of stars above us, the lights of Watford in the distance, the occasional rumble of the North Western Railway breaking the deep stillness. The freshness of the spring mornings, the beauty of the flowering shrubs, the scent of azaleas, of lilacs, of syringas and roses. The wonderful coolness of the hall as one came in out of the glare of an August sun. These, and many other memories, will stay with me until I die, and perhaps afterwards —who knows?"

The other quotation is from Charles Lamb, who mourns a lost Paradise in Hertfordshire:

"Mine, too, whose else, thy costly fruit garden with the sun-baked wall; the ampler pleasure gardens . . . and stretching still beyond in old formality thy firry wilderness, the haunt of the squirrel and the day-long murmuring wood pigeon, with that antique image in the centre, God or Goddess I wist not. But child of Athens and of old Rome paid never a sincerer worship to Pan or to Sylvanus in their native groves than I do that frag-mental mystery. Was it for this that I kissed my childish hands too fervently in your idol worship, walks and windings of Blakes-moor; for this or what sin of mine has the plough passed over your pleasant places? I sometimes think that as men when they die do not die at all, so of their extinguished habitations there may be a hope or germ to be revivified."

3

MOOR PARK, BY CAROLINE GROSVENOR[1]

I HAD come from a large and uproarious family, closely packed in a moderate-sized London house, and at first I greatly appre-ciated the sense of space, of dignity, of orderliness. For large and heterogeneous as was often the company assembled, its size seemed to preclude any sense of crowd, while nothing disturbed the routine—and the unvarying precision with which the sequence of domestic events followed each other, like the most immutable of natural laws.

Later on, when I had lived there for a few years, this unvary-ing routine, carried out for the most part by a large staff of

[1] *Née* Caroline Stuart Wortley.

well-fed but much-bored retainers, grew to oppress me, and I found myself longing for a life of far less ease but of greater variety and colour.

To the newcomer the most impressive characteristic of the life at Moor Park was that a whole grown-up family of sons and daughters, some of whom were married and with children of their own, lived together in one house. The eldest son "Bo,"[1] had, it is true, a house of his own, but every summer for several months he and his wife and all his children made their home under the paternal roof. My two sisters-in-law, the daughters of the house, had reached middle age without its having ever apparently occurred to them to start homes of their own. They migrated with their parents from Moor Park to London and back again to Moor Park, twice yearly. To a certain extent they had made a life of their own among their neighbours both rich and poor, but they were essentially dependent on their parents, and had nominally neither control nor freedom.

Of the four other sons only one had gone out completely into the world. This was the second son, Thomas, always called Tommy, who was following the career of a diplomatist in distant lands—though he, too, accompanied by his wife, sometimes came back for long spells of time. Norman, the third son, who had served for five or six years in the Grenadier Guards, and had later sat in Parliament for Chester, still clung with deep attachment to his home life, though, immersed as he was in music and in books, he certainly sat very light to it. Algy and Dick, the former an ex-officer in the Rifle Brigade, the latter a barrister, while both made frequent excursions into the outer world, each still had his room kept for him both in London and at Moor Park, returning between flights to the parental nest.

It was in this community or hierarchy (shall we say?) that the daughters-in-law, brought in from outside, had to take their place as best they could. For a hierarchy it certainly was, every member knowing and keeping his or her place in pain of instant reproof and strong disapproval. At the head were, of course,

[1] Robert, afterwards 2nd Baron Ebury.

my father and mother-in-law, Lord and Lady Ebury. "His Lordship" (as we all called him, or to his face "Lordship") I think
thoroughly enjoyed his position as head of his little kingdom,
taking life very easily and assuming, except when occasionally
forced to take notice of some unpleasant fact, that all was for
the best in the best possible of worlds. His favourite expression
was, "We must just do the best we can," and this usually meant,
"Let us do nothing at all." To "her Ladyship" he left all the
care of that great house with its strangely assorted population
of sons and daughters, of daughters-in-law and their children,
with their retinues of tutors, governesses and nurses, maids and
valets, and the difficulties and *tracasseries* innumerable which continually arose. His Lordship, though over eighty when I first
saw him (he lived to ninety-three), was vigorous for his age,
spare in figure, abstemious in his habits, very fond of a game of
billiards in the afternoon and a rubber of whist in the evening.
He was decidedly deaf, but often used his deafness as a convenient
way of evading difficulties. Indeed, he always seemed to me a
past master in the avoidance of the unpleasant in life, a quality
which must have been useful in his diplomatic career in youth,
and later in the post which he held in the household of the Prince
Consort. He was unvaryingly good-humoured and kind, very
fond of doing little kindnesses and giving small presents, very
genial and ready for a joke. Needless to say, he was immensely
popular in the neighbourhood—far more than either his wife or
daughters, though they gave immeasurably more time and
trouble to the welfare of the people in Rickmansworth and on
the estate.

It would probably be difficult to find a character in every way
more unlike his than that of my mother-in-law.[1] While the
key-note of the one was easy-going and *laisser-faire*, the key-note
of the other was intensity of feeling—intensity of love for those
few she admitted to her love—intensity of will to live up to her
own high ideal of life. She accused herself always of having a
very hot temper, and she could undoubtedly be formidable when
angry, but I never saw her give way to it for trivial reasons,

[1] See page 109.

though it was obvious that many of the details of her burden-
some and monotonous life wearied her to the point of exasperation. An Irishwoman by birth, she hated the solidity, the grandeur,
the respectability of the life of which the burden fell almost
entirely on her frail shoulders. She longed for freedom—freedom to hear music, to play with children, to kneel for hours in
church or sit up with a dying woman—yet she was always in
her place at meals or punctual for any of the small functions and
ceremonies which so pleased and amused "his Lordship" and
were so infinitely tedious to her. In stature she was very small,
and for the last years of her life much bent, so that at a distance
her figure leaning on a stick had a rather witch-like appearance,
which was accentuated by the extreme shabbiness of her clothes.
For on herself she would spend nothing, economising and saving
in every possible way in order to give some really valuable gift
to someone she loved.

But the witch-like impression of which I spoke was dispelled
the instant she raised her face and one saw the delicately cut
features, the long eyes, and, most of all, the wonderful skin which
to the last day of her life retained the colour and texture of
a child's.

An amusing incident in connection with the shabbiness of
"her Ladyship's" appearance took place when I was staying at
my brother-in-law Reggie Talbot's house in Grosvenor Street.
I had been ill, and "her Ladyship" came to inquire after me.
The door was opened by my brother-in-law's soldier servant,
one Harvey, a cavalryman of some six feet four inches in height,
but with no corresponding size of brains. Seeing this small figure
in a poke bonnet and the shabbiest of old black waterproofs,
with black cotton gloves much too long in the fingers clasping
a large but very plain umbrella, he told her without more ado
to go to the back door—"she had no business there!" Her Ladyship said nothing, but going back to 35 Park Street, my father-
in-law's town house, fetched her card-case, and returning walked
down the area steps to the back door, and was once more con-
fronted by Harvey, to whom she presented her card. The unfortunate man rushed to confess his *gaffe* to my sister's maid, who

described him as "white in the face and all of a tremble." Lady Ebury often related the incident with infinite amusement. She always enjoyed a joke against herself and her dignity. She often referred to herself as an old "picture card." Nevertheless, she could be very much the *grande dame*, and I can imagine no one with whom it was less easy to take a liberty. Looking back, I feel her to have been one of the rarest and most interesting people I have ever known.

Next in importance in the hierarchy came my two elderly sisters-in-law, Siss and B., Victoria and Albertine Grosvenor. Siss was the eldest of the family and about twelve years older than B., who looked up to and adored her to the last as a creature of a superior mould. Siss, though from early youth she had laboured under the misfortune of being enormously fat, was a person of considerable ability and force, and I had constantly the impression that she felt her powers shackled and restricted and her energy wasted in the life she led. Under her father's geniality of manner she concealed a very strong ego, and would like to have ruled us with a rod of iron. The laws of the hierarchy, however, forbade this, and she confined herself to keeping a watchful eye on any encroachments by her sisters-in-law on her or her parents' prerogatives. Between her and Minnie,[1] Bo's wife, there were many passages of arms. As the wife of the eldest son, Minnie met her on equal terms, and as her character was as forceful and her ego even stronger than Siss's, it was a case of Greek meeting Greek. Siss, it must be said, was genuinely devoted to her mother, and to spare her possible worry, I think, often gave way. Siss had a real gift for music, and trained the choir and played the organ in church most competently and well. Her other taste was for driving. She had an ugly and (to my mind) inconvenient pony-carriage, shaped like a low dog-cart on four wheels, in which I have seen her drive three ponies abreast, and I was told that she had formerly driven a team of four donkeys. She drove remarkably well, and had a thorough understanding of horses. She would take her pony-carriage out in all weathers, and often late in the evening when choir practices

[1] *Née* the Honble. Emily White, daughter of Lord Annaly.

123

or church services necessitated her presence. Like her mother, she allowed no personal inconvenience or fatigue to interfere with what she thought to be her duty.

This last characteristic was shared to the full by B., who, indeed, carried it to almost extravagant lengths. She had none of Siss's egotism, but she had an unfathomable store of quiet obstinacy. To dissuade B. from doing something she thought right, on the ground of expediency, however urgent, was like trying to move the Great Pyramid. Even Siss would shrug her shoulders in despair when B. set off to walk to Rickmansworth and back in the snow, for some cause which to all of us seemed inadequate—or deprived herself of some cherished outing because she thought she ought to stay with her father, who did not in the least want her. If one attempted to argue with her she rubbed her hands together very hard and changed the subject. B. carried unselfishness to a point at which it became a vice, and I used to tell her that it was an insult to those she lived with, to assume that they wished her constantly to sacrifice her pleasure and well-being to theirs. B. was not clever, and had inherited from her mother her intensity of character and will, without the latter's saving humour and charm. But she was the stuff of which saints and fanatics are made—uncomfortable stuff for human nature's daily needs.

The four persons I have described above were the most permanent elements in the patriarchal life of Moor Park. The rest of us were all to some extent floating population, though Norman and I were more permanent than any of the others. Algy and Dick made meteoric appearances and disappearances, and it was an understood thing that we never asked them where they had been, though they sometimes told us unasked.

Living in a large and heterogeneous community necessitates many unwritten laws, against which being young and inexperienced I must often blunderingly have transgressed. One of the most important of these was the avoidance of certain topics, more especially at meal times or other gatherings of the whole family. Of these topics probably the most dangerous was religion, on which subject the family was sharply divided into three camps.

My father-in-law was very Low Church, had in past times
strongly advocated the revision of the Prayer Book, and now
supported very Low Church societies and their activities. My
mother-in-law, Siss, B., and Minnie were all very High Church.
Unknown to "his Lordship" they stole out to early Communion,
when possible attended week-day services, took in High Church
periodicals, and even concealed crucifixes in remote corners of
their bedrooms. All the younger male members of the family,
except Bo (who went to church but mocked impartially at High
and Low Church practices), were open free-thinkers. Later on,
when Algy married, his wife Queenie,[1] being a Roman Catholic,
brought in another variety of religious belief, but I think it was
almost entirely the High Church members in the party who
made the discussion of any subject, even remotely connected
with religion, unsafe. His Lordship would have been willing
enough to live and let live, contenting himself with mildly chaff-
ing his wife and daughters about their ritualistic tendencies. Even
the regrettable opinions of his sons, though they troubled him
occasionally, had never caused him to lie awake at night, or
otherwise ruffled the calm of his existence. He contented himself with praying for them in the course of family prayers, read
by him in the big hall, among the strange setting of heathen
gods and goddesses, on Sunday evenings as well as on every week-
day morning. These extempore prayers, interpolated always when
the subject of them was present and kneeling with his elbows on
one of the red leather chairs in a peculiarly defenceless position,
were I am sure a great satisfaction to his Lordship, who, under
the cloak of a petition to the Deity, could thus safely admonish
his recalcitrant children.

But to her Ladyship, Siss, and B., Low Church and free-thinking
opinions were distressing to the point of agony. They could brook
no trifling with them, and I have seen B. get up and leave the
luncheon table because his Lordship, who had a strong element
of the tease in him, had made some joke or allusion which
she thought unbecoming. This love of teasing had been inherited
to a very high degree by Bo, who could at times be merciless,

[1] *Née* Dorothy Simeon, daughter of Sir John Simeon.

125

and to some extent also, by Norman, Algy and Dick. The two last loved above all things to sail near the wind, and to keep us in a twitter of anxiety as to what they would say next. Not only were religious subjects taboo, but anything verging on the improper was anathema to my spinster sisters-in-law. Algy, deaf, good-humoured, but full of a sort of light-hearted mischievousness, was quite impervious to the impatient tappings of Siss's foot under the table, or the frenzied rubbing of B.'s hands, accompanied by high-pitched efforts to change the subject. The effect on me (and this was no doubt a factor in Algy's enjoyment) was an irresistible longing to laugh, which if given way to ranged me at once on the side of the miscreants, and brought on me dire, if unexpressed, disapproval. Then there were certain things not to be mentioned before the servants, and others which were supposed to be kept from his Lordship in order not to worry him, though I always shrewdly suspected that he knew all about them and did not in the least mean to worry. Altogether conversation at meal times was like navigation through a narrow channel filled with sunken rocks. The result was, of course, that certain safe but not exciting topics were worn threadbare—such as the weather, the dogs, and the various forms of exercise resorted to by the members of the family, walking, riding, driving, as the case might be. These last two were, however, not free from possibilities of disagreement, as a certain friction was always latent between Siss on the one hand and her brothers on the other regarding the management and control of the stables. Siss had a laudable desire to protect coachmen, stablemen, and horses from overwork, which merged at times into the less laudable desire to keep all those surrounding her on leading strings, while her brothers acutely resented her interference, and thought, as did most of us, that it was the exact opposite of overwork from which the men and horses of the Moor Park establishment were likely to suffer.

4

MOOR PARK, BY MARGARET PEYTON-JONES

I AM in the difficult position of trying to describe the pictures in a picture-gallery rather than narrate well-remembered incidents.

The most vivid picture in my mind is that of the nursery which Susie and I shared. It was a big room (it always seemed to me to be positively vast) situated at the N.E. corner of the top floor, with four big windows on two sides, with deep window seats, on which I used to love to sit and look out at the garden beneath, or across the valley at the hazy view of the Rickmansworth water-meadows beyond.

Especially do I remember the look of the valley in a winter's evening when the snow was on the ground, the black trees rising on either side, and the white expanse between flooded with the faint glow of the winter sunset, which gradually faded as night came on to a blue which also seemed to glow but with something magic in the light.

I do not remember very much about the furniture of the nursery, excepting the chairs. These consisted of three or four armchairs made of wood, painted with garlands of flowers on a dark green background, and with delicate cane seats. I loved these chairs, but this didn't prevent me kicking my feet against them just for the fun of the thing. I have since realised that they were particularly exquisite examples of Hepplewhite's art.

On opening the nursery door, one emerged on to a long, wide passage leading to the opposite end of the house: the carpet was of an early Victorian pattern, a mingling of bright blue and red, and of the thick noise-muffling description, which was lucky considering how much noisy scamperings it had to muffle. A few yards down the passage a smaller passage curved off to the right to where the suite of rooms occupied by Auntie Siss and Auntie B. were situated. I did not very often enter these rooms, as I have to confess that I was not *persona grata* with my two old aunts: but I remember vividly a dressing-table set of an opaque turquoise blue glass which adorned Auntie B.'s table, and which seemed to me wonderfully charming and desirable.

Between the main passage and these rooms was situated that place of fascinating mystery, the box-room—to be accurate, it was two or three rooms leading out of one another—and I have no sort of doubt that when my instinct told me that it contained all sorts of hidden treasures, it was perfectly right, though the treasures were not perhaps of the sort that would appeal to a small child.

I think the room must have been lit by a skylight, for it seemed always to be suffused by a dusty golden light, fading all round the sides to mysterious gloom. I do not remember ever finding any treasures to reward my searches, but it was one of my greatest joys to be allowed to hunt over the huge old trunks, the wooden boxes, baskets, cases, bags, and disused furniture, that this room contained, for hope sprang eternal!

Every evening after tea, Susie and I came down to our mother's room for an hour before bed-time. I can vividly remember the look of the room, with its huge glowing fire (it seems to be always winter in my recollections!) which I think cast more light on the furniture than the lamps or the soft yellow candle-light that was supposed to illumine the room. How well I can see the huge fourposter bed, the writing-table in front of the sofa, at the end of the bed, the dainty muslin-skirted dressing-table, on which reposed, among other things, the curling tongs which I so deeply envied, and of which I am supposed to have said to Mother that "when I'm grown up, and you dead, I shall have those tongs."

At the left of the fireplace was a door leading into Aunt Sophie's room—a room very like mother's in size, shape and furniture, and which, owing to the kindness of its occupant, we invaded just as confidently as we did that of our mother.

The rest of the rooms on this floor consisted of the bedrooms allotted to the various other members of the family when they visited Moor Park, and the many spare bedrooms for the use of the frequent guests of my grandparents. Many of them had hand-painted Chinese papers on the walls.

I must not leave this floor without showing the gallery that ran round the top of the central hall. This gallery had slender gilded wooden rails, and at each of the four corners was poised a huge lamp, like a great glass urn with top of carved and gilded wood, which always shook ominously as we ran past. I can still remember my mother's terror as we pounded at full speed round the gallery, lest we should slip on the polished oak floor and crash through the frail railing on to the marble floor some thirty feet beneath! The walls of the gallery were painted in grey monochrome, with allegorical figures standing in painted niches, each holding one of the Signs of the Zodiac! They always seemed to me very ghostly and god-like.

At either end of the gallery, through a very high doorway, was a flight of stairs. The one near mother's bedroom was the grand cedar staircase, with again the gilt and glass urns at each turn of the banisters. The staircase on the opposite side was the real flight of stone steps leading from the very top of the house to the very bottom, and the fact principally connected in my mind with this staircase was when my beloved Sarah (the head housemaid and my especial friend and benefactor) slipped down a whole flight, cutting open her forehead, and causing her to be laid up for weeks with concussion of the brain.

On the ground floor these two staircases both led through big double doors, into the marble entrance hall—a place that appears so limitlessly vast in my memory that I feel more as if I were trying to describe a landscape than a space enclosed within four walls.

Six doors led into the hall, the two I have already mentioned, the front door, the saloon door opposite, and the doors leading into the dining-room and grandpapa's room, both opposite each other, and in a line with the staircase doors: between these latter doors were ranged on either side of the wall two very long carved and gilded settees with seats and backs of bright red leather. How well I can remember the smell of that leather as I buried my aching face in it at family prayers—aching because of the agonising tension of trying to keep my mouth shut and so prevent the wild giggles from escaping. Those family prayers cannot have been as funny as they seemed to me to be. But perhaps even at my early age the fact of the naked gods and goddesses, whose pictures adorned the walls, looking down upon the backs of my kneeling aunts, and the rest of the rather curiously assorted company, struck me as incongruous, though probably it was just the inevitable tendency in the child to laugh when laughter is taboo.

I cannot close this account without a word about the huge labyrinthine basement, in which, when my Nanny and I were alone at Moor Park, I often spent many happy hours, the echoing stone passages, with their confusing numbers of stone staircases leading to the upper floor (whose geography I never mastered), the delicious "frowst" of the housekeeper's room, the pungent, aromatic smell of the old-fashioned still-room, and a small room where Sarah, the head housemaid, and one or two other favoured mortals had their meals, where occasionally I received snacks of cheese, a dainty I specially loved, and heaven knows what else besides.

The nicest exit was through the window of the saloon leading down some steps to the lovely Italian garden running the full length of the house, with its dark cypress trees, and beds with clipped box borders. Further away, down a slope, and past the lawn with its sweet briar hedge, was the long terrace with a carved stone seat at either end, and a stone balustrade with stone urns at intervals running the length of it, with some vivid yellow creeping plant growing over the stone-work.

Retracing our steps, past the round azalea bed (how divine it used to smell!), through the Italian garden, we should come to a wrought-iron gate coloured blue-green which led out on to the path to the pleasure ground. Never was a place better named! It was indeed a pleasure ground, with its mysterious round pond surrounded by dense masses of rhododendrons, and reflecting on its waters a Greek temple which stood on a green slope above it, and which always had a splendidly pagan air. Peacocks strutted everywhere and broke the silence with their strange call, and beyond was the little wood where, in the spring, masses of daffodils always bloomed. Looking back, the place seems to me to have had a curious charmed atmosphere, almost a haunted one, but if so the spirits must have been gay and happy ones for the place was never sad.

The impressions of a small child, where the human race is concerned, must necessarily be like a rather distorted snapshot, but here are some of the people who made up the background of my important young life, as they appeared to me. Grandpapa was very, very tall and thin, always in black, his face seemed carved out of ivory, and he had two little semicircular curls that came in front of his ears. I always felt him benign and well-disposed. Our grandmother I can remember very little—except that she was very small and bunched up, and always in black, and that she did not seem always well-disposed (in this I fancy I was right, for I was far from being her favourite).

My uncles I recall chiefly as well-meaning people who flitted in and out of life at Moor Park, and whom I principally remember during the skating on the round pond, when they performed wonderful feats. My mother used to implore me to keep out of their way, for they would certainly have run over me, to our mutual detriment, before they had ever realised my insignificant existence. These were my relations as they then appeared to me, but the people who really filled my life were my dear old Nanny, and Sarah the head housemaid, already mentioned, those kindest of friends who bestowed so much love and understanding upon me—and who always tried to stand between me and the law. Then there was funny, crusty old Soey, who made such wonderful patchwork quilts, and who once deigned to instruct me in the art; old Lideard the butler, who used to love to ring the luncheon gong as loud as he could when I passed in order to see how much the sound terrified me; Mrs. Allet, an old paralysed woman, and Mrs. Lacey who had in times past worked at Moor Park, who both lived in cottages in Betchworth Heath and whom we used regularly to visit; and a score of other people —keepers, gardeners, coachmen, lodge-keepers, who were always kind and good-natured to us children.

Looking back at it all from present day conditions, life at Moor Park under the old régime seems to me as remote as if it had taken place in the reign of Queen Anne. But in my memory of it, it is composed entirely of beauty, happiness and romance, and to this day, if I want to call up a vision of these qualities at their very highest expression, I have only to whisper to myself the words—Moor Park.

5

THE EBURYS IN LONDON

WHEN they were in London my grandparents lived at 35 Park Street, in a corner house which overlooked the garden at Grosvenor House at the back. I can just remember the staircase curving up from a dark hall. There was a tall, stained-glass window beside it and a mosaic pavement on the spacious landing. I can recall a big, dignified drawing-room, and a bare shabby nursery at the top of the house where we stayed once or twice.

For many years (in fact, until not long ago) there was a fair-sized looking-glass outside the front door of 35 Park Street. This has often puzzled passers-by, as a looking-glass outside a house is not often met with in London. It was put up by my grandmother Charlotte Ebury for a good reason. Her mother[1] Lady Cowley ran away (as the saying was in those days) with Lord Anglesey. Lord Cowley married again. My grandmother was devoted to her mother and to her stepmother. Both of them paid her long and frequent visits after she married my grandfather. She was disturbed by the fear that their visits might coincide, and could not face the embarrassment that this would cause. She therefore hit upon the device of putting a looking-glass outside the front door, and she received whichever of the two ladies, mother or stepmother, who came to see her, in a sitting-room next to the hall on the ground floor. If a carriage

[1] *Née* Lady Charlotte Cadogan. She married Henry Wellesley, afterwards Lord Cowley. He divorced her and she married Henry, 1st Marquess of Anglesey.

132

was heard to drive up in the street outside, a peep in the looking-glass revealed the identity of the visitor. If it reflected the last person she wanted to see at the moment, she told the butler to say that she was not at home.

There was a story that my grandfather walked home from the House of Lords with an acquaintance who did not know his name. As they were preparing to part company at the end of Park Street this gentlemen remarked, pointing to No. 35, "You see that house there? It belongs to Lord Ebury. He must be an unlucky man; he's got two mothers-in-law."

35 Park Street was sold after my grandfather's death. I can just remember the hatchment that was put up on the house, after he died, and during his illness the acres of straw (as it seemed to me) in Park Street to deaden the noise of passing vehicles. My grandfather was over ninety and stone deaf when he died, so that noise cannot have mattered to him; but straw was always put down in streets where anyone was ill who could afford this luxury. Our forebears had an extraordinary sensitiveness to noise. Edward Lear constantly complains in his letters of his annoyance at hearing a man digging with pick and shovel in the road, or a distant piano being played, and Thomas Carlyle nearly drove his wife mad by his insistence on having a sound-proof room in their house in Chelsea.

When my grandfather died the old régime went completely, and my uncle found that he had to make a clearance of a great many of the ancient retainers at Moor Park. Endless waste and extravagance was uncovered, and he had a hard time pulling things round. We still visited Moor Park, and I loved the place as much as ever, but the old glamour was gone from the people there.

My uncle and aunt were formidable people and hard to get on with. Uncle Bo, as we called him, was an extremely able man of business, and was chairman of the Army and Navy Stores for many years. He was cold and sarcastic, asking us children cutting little questions, and listening to our answers with condescending amusement. We got out of his way as much as possible.

His wife, Aunt Minnie, was very handsome with lovely warm colouring and a graceful figure. She had the prettiest laugh I have ever heard; when she threw back her head and laughed, you had to laugh too. But she laughed very seldom, and her moods were unpredictable. She could cajole anyone, but she was subject to fierce irritations and sudden angers. In her youth she had been a fine horsewoman and a friend of the ill-starred Empress of Austria. She and her husband had had for many years a house at Brackley in Northamptonshire where they moved in the strictest set of fox-hunting society. Looking back I seem to realise that her life was rather a lonely one. She was very High Church and fond of elaborate ritual. I hope that her religion comforted her, though no one can be sure of this for anyone else.

My father all through my childhood used a bedroom on the top floor of Moor Park as a sitting-room. I remember it as piled with books and music and strongly scented with tobacco. My aunt turned this little room into a chapel where it smelt faintly of matting and flowers. Her daughter, Alice, and I (as children) were sent out to gather some flowers for the altar. Chattering earnestly to each other, we discovered some white blooms that we thought very pretty, and it was only when we handed them to Aunt Minnie that we were sharply ordered to throw them away, as they were wild garlic. We were talking so hard that we had never noticed their pungent scent.

My mother was the friend and confidante of the Ebury sons and daughters. There was a lack of pretension and snobbery about my parents and an easiness in our house which they liked. Hughie Grosvenor was specially devoted to my mother. We children did not care for him. He was not at all interested in us, and he looked, we thought, sneering, with his dark smiling face and small black moustache.

Hughie was in the Diplomatic Service. He showed a special aptitude for learning languages. It was said that he gained a knowledge of Mandarin Chinese, when he was in Pekin, more quickly than any British diplomat had previously done. I believe that the polished sophistication of his manner did not please some

134

of the people with whom he came in contact, but he went ahead in his profession none the less. Unluckily he was a gambler, and his father, who had had to work hard and economise hard when he succeeded to his inheritance, was very angry when he realised what Hughie was doing. He paid Hughie's debts once, but said with complete finality that he would never do so again.

Gamblers can seldom stop gambling. Hughie lost a lot ot money and, afraid to face his father, shot himself in Vienna. It is strange to think that one of my own blood and kin lies in a cemetery in Vienna. Perhaps his grave has been broken up by bombing, perhaps it is in the Russian zone. I do not know. All that is left of this enigmatic, brilliant boy, is a graceful hand mirror which lies on my dressing-table. Hughie brought it from Pekin and gave it to my mother.

Bertie, his elder brother, had no strong characteristics or aptitudes. Maudie, who married Maurice Glyn, was graceful and charming. She read voraciously and had great independence of mind. Alice was lovely, and she had not only beauty but such gaiety and charm that she could have persuaded anyone, I verily believe, to do anything she wanted them to do. She married Ivor Guest, the second Lord Wimborne, and became hostess to the Liberal Party and for a time Vicereine of Ireland.

At the end of the family came Francis. In his youth he went out to ranch in Canada, and even now on the walls of small Western homes you will see his photograph, and people still talk of him there.

In the first decades of the twentieth century, the Canadian West was magnetic to a certain type of Englishman, and Francis's special qualities were suited to a life of hard work and adventure. In 1914 he joined up in a Canadian regiment and showed great qualities of leadership in the hard fighting of that war. He was tall and handsome, with a nose that recalled his ancestor's, the Iron Duke. He returned to England, succeeded his brother as Lord Ebury, became Chairman of the Army and Navy Stores, and spent his spare time in the winter hunting in the shires, for he was a hard, and even reckless, rider to hounds.

His death at the age of forty-eight from the results of a

hunting accident, took away someone who left a real blank in
the English scene. I always felt that if you had known Francis,
you would have some idea of what the men were like who
rode with Rupert of the Rhine, at Edgehill.

The Army and Navy Stores, through the Eburys, father and
son, has always been a great shopping centre for my family.
I remember it mostly as dark and rather cosy, and as selling
miraculously cheap and good wares. Maudie Glyn once said to
me that she was glad that Hugh Walpole had (in one of his
novels) put in an episode about a bishop's wife who goes to the
Stores to buy a hot-water bottle, and spends a large part of the
afternoon doing this and looking at carpets. "It is nice," said
Maudie, "to think that the atmosphere of the old Stores has been
described once and for all." Shops have changed so much in the
last few years and so completely lost their separate identities, that
it is pleasant to recall how in my youth (in fact up to the twenties
in this century) none of the big London shops were standardised;
all had their own separate idiosyncrasies in what they sold and
how they sold it. They then had more faith in their customers
than they have now, for customers in those days knew what was
good, and what was going to last and go on looking nice in the
matter of clothes or textiles. Flashy things did not appeal to them,
nor did anything which was remotely standardised, and the big
shops catered for differences in taste. It must have been (so far
as selling was concerned) more interesting to serve a few people
who knew what they wanted. I often feel sorry for shopkeepers
and assistants now as crowds of haggard-looking people snatch
at inferior goods at three times their pre-war price. Anyone who
cares for the finesse of their job must find this frustrating and
tedious.

I am sitting in the library at Elsfield on a cold July day in
1951. Outside the library windows, rain is coming down in
sheets. I suppose that it will be good for the garden, but it will
scatter the roses which are in full bloom. The weather supports
my feeling that much is despoiled and sad, and it makes my

thoughts wander back into the past. When I read what I have
written about Moor Park, I feel that I am like a traveller who
long ago visited a far country, and who many years afterwards
found it hard to believe that he had ever passed that way.

The life at Moor Park seems a little like a ballet. My small
and lovely grandmother, my tall grandfather, the charming, careless uncles, my father with his secret world of music, the servants
with their separate idiosyncrasies; the horses and the stable men,
the cricket, the skating, the visitors, all appear in my recollection to be revolving to some far-off music conceived on some
definite plan or pattern. I know that this was not so and that
my family were real people, who lived the jerky and uneven
lives lived by all human beings.

I know that my mother chafed under the pinpricks of family
life at Moor Park. She went away gladly to a small house in
London, 58 Green Street, which she had made charming and
homelike. My father loved it too, and we children liked it, but
thought London a very poor substitute for Moor Park. We had
a little courtyard in which stood two plane trees, and we made
ourselves as black as chimney sweeps playing beneath them, and
this soothed our nostalgia a little.

One of the excitements of the week at 58 Green Street was
the arrival of the carrier with his horse-drawn covered cart. He
brought my mother a hamper of fruit and vegetables. Vegetables
bored us, as they do all children, but the flowers we looked at
with delight as they brought a whiff of scent from Moor Park.

As I have said, we moved to 30 Upper Grosvenor Street. It
was a tall, narrow house with two staircases, most inconvenient
by modern standards. It had a covered passage which ran along
by the side of a flagged courtyard to a very light and pleasant
kitchen, which had every advantage except that of nearness to
the dining-room. On a balcony stood a round green tub in which
flourished a myrtle bush. It had been grown from a cutting from
my grandmother Charlotte Ebury's wedding bouquet. I had a
spray of this myrtle in my bouquet when I was married.

30 Upper Grosvenor Street was a house which had both
dignity and beauty. We looked out on Hyde Park and a sort

of Palladian outcrop at the end of the long wall of Grosvenor House consisting of a pediment and pillars. We lived under the wing of the ducal mansion next door, and the comings and goings of the Westminsters[1] were of great interest to us children. I remember as a highlight of childhood going to a dancing class at Grosvenor House. I can recall nothing about the dancing, but I have never forgotten the iced lemonade and cakes which were given when the class was over. I suppose that all our years of food austerity have made us remember the good things we once had, but I feel a little ashamed that I can only remember what I ate at a party to which I was taken at a house which forms the end of Stratford Place. The hostess was remarkably attractive and the house must have looked beautiful, but, like a needle steadily pointing north, I can only remember two wonderful lemon ices which I devoured. I have eaten the most exquisite and delicate ices on two continents, but they never came near in their ambrosial quality to the two I had in that house in Stratford Place.

Grosvenor House has now been forgotten, and I am one of the few people who can remember it. It was not a high house, but it had dignified and spacious rooms done up in white and gold. The two famous pictures, The Blue Boy and Mrs. Siddons, were well hung, and we gazed at them with admiration; but my childish interest centred on the sedan chair in the hall. I longed to get into it, but did not dare suggest this.

The Westminsters were always kind, and we went to stay with them at Eaton Hall near Chester. I felt as if I had stepped into the Arabian Nights. Great chandeliers trembled and flashed in the rooms and passages. There were tall liveried footmen, and a great deal of gilding and red velvet. It had none of the mellow beauty of Moor Park, in fact I can recall someone saying of cousin Westminster that he had a great deal of taste but that it was all bad—not quite true, as there were a great many beautiful objects at Eaton. But the trembling lights, the footmen, the gilding and the carpets, into which small feet comfortably sank, appealed to a childish snobbery in me, and for years a member

[1] Hugh Lupus Grosvenor, 1st Duke of Westminster.

of my family cherished a letter written by me in which I described
our visit to Eaton in the richest vein of *The Young Visiters*.

When my father died, my sister and I were sent to sleep in
Grosvenor House, accompanied by a maid. The family were
away and the rooms on the ground floor were dust-sheeted and
ghostly. I remember my despairing misery when I woke in the
morning. The ceiling of the bedroom was covered with stout
cupids who disported themselves in unreal clouds against an azure
background. They wavered and dissolved before my tear-dimmed
eyes. Grosvenor House had little architectural beauty, but it had
charm and dignity, and the garden, which sloped down to a
high wall at the back, was green and pleasant and full of pigeons.

Meg Grosvenor[1] used to come and see us before she married,
and I have a memory that she once took a rabbit out of her pocket,
for she kept livestock on the terrace of Grosvenor House. (If it
was not a rabbit, it was a kitten.) We children thought this a
lovable and delightful trait in a visitor, as most people who
visited one's parents carried nothing more interesting in their
hands than a sharp-edged ivory card case with a monogram on it.

Ladies in those days had black velvet, silver-mounted bags
attached to their waists in which they carried spectacles and
handkerchiefs austerely scented with eau de Cologne. I imagine
that the contents of the large bags which we all carry now would
have surprised them. Our "make-up" sets they would have
regarded with horror. I suppose I was still rather old-fashioned,
but I remember being surprised about 1918 when someone lunch-
ing at our house took out a battery of make-up, and proceeded
to attend to her face in public. I had plenty of powder in my
dressing-table upstairs, but I had never done up my face when
other people were present.

In my girlhood we were allowed few aids to beauty. If our
faces shone, they shone. We had small booklets of so-called *papier
poudré* which exhaled a rather sickly smell. We rubbed a parsi-
monious quota of powder on to our noses and must have presented
an odd streaky appearance. Women who put on much make-up
would have been considered fast by my grandmother and aunts,

[1] Afterwards Marchioness of Cambridge.

and although some famous beauties did make up after their first youth was gone, this was critically commented upon and not admired. I should say that the art of make-up was imperfectly understood, and women were apt to plaster too much rouge and eye-black on their faces and that the whole effect was rather obvious and crude. I smile to think what the people of those old days would have said about the modern young woman who makes up a huge mouth in a startling pillar-box red. This I am sure would have been considered not only ugly but as showing a strongly immoral tendency. In fact, to make a bad pun, women of their generation wore their rouge with a difference.

PART IV
A Wedding

A WEDDING

VICTORIAN novels had a way of ending with wedding bells, and it is, perhaps, not out of place to end this book about the last portion of the nineteenth century and some few years of this one, with an account of my own wedding.

Weddings now do not seem to be very different to weddings in those days. There is still the white-clad bride who often wears a sparkling tiara instead of one made of the traditional orange blossom, but otherwise looks much the same. Bridegrooms are smart and nervously make conversation to the best man. Brides-maids have wreaths and flowing dresses, and there is usually a minute page who bursts into tears and seeks refuge with a friendly grown-up. The same music is played, and the exhortations to the bride and bridegroom sound strangely familiar.

We were married in St. George's, Hanover Square, which was then a fashionable church, to be married there suggesting rank and money. Our financial prospects were not of opulence, but my mother very sensibly said that St. George's was our parish church and that it was better to be married there than to go further afield. She added that it had a wide aisle and roomy pews from which the guests could see the ceremony in comfort.

I went there the other day. The church looked much the same and it still has the charm and elegance which pseudo-gothic buildings entirely lack.

There is one great difference between the weddings of to-day and the weddings of yesterday. The wedding receptions of to-day are held in hotels, which still strikes me as chill and impersonal. There was a friendliness and a personal charm about a wedding party in the house of the bride's parents which is now absent.

However, there is no doubt there are fewer possibilities of friction between the bride's and bridegroom's families if the arrangements are made by caterers and hotel managements.

All families look at things from different points of view. My mother and my future mother-in-law did not see eye to eye on some things. John's mother was anxious to have a wedding group photograph taken at 30 Upper Grosvenor Street. My mother, after much thought and anxious consultation with her sisters, decided against this. She could not see her way to its being done, she said. The guests would arrive while the photograph was being taken, they would be bored, or, worse still, they might even go away. People in Scotland might like to have wedding groups, but she doubted if it was ever done in London.

I cannot help smiling now at the thought of this episode. Wedding groups are now a feature of every wedding, and I wish that I had a photograph that I could take out of a drawer and look at; though perhaps it is just as well that I have not, as it would bring much sadness in its train. I should look with sorrow at my cousin Rosamund Grosvenor (she married Jack Lynch afterwards) as she would have stood, graceful and charming in her pink bridesmaid's dress, holding a small basket of flowers. She was killed by a flying bomb in the second of the great wars which our generation has endured, and four of my other bridesmaids have died. It is better to have no photographs.

I remember some episodes of my wedding party that stand out with a sharp clarity. We were to spend our honeymoon in Hampshire at Tylney Hall, lent to us by the Lionel Phillips. When we went away the hall at 30 Upper Grosvenor Street was filled with wedding guests who were much entertained by the parting between myself and a strange but beloved parrot which had some years before been brought from Australia by my aunt Margaret Talbot. Aglavaine, as we called him, was a very odd looking bird. He had a commanding upper beak and a mass of wrinkled grey skin round a pair of bright dark eyes. In spite of his formidable appearance, he was a gentle and affectionate bird who had no objection to being kissed. Our ancient parlourmaid carried him into the hall wrapped in a clean towel from which his grotesque head emerged, so that he should not spoil my pale blue "going away" dress. My fond embrace and his frantic struggles to emerge from the constricting towel added a welcome touch of farce to the leavetaking from my girlhood's home.

A Wedding

Even so, our wedding was no doubt, in the eyes of some of the guests, very like the one they had been to the week before. Some of them asked (I was told) in audible whispers, who was this young Scotsman who was marrying a girl they had known all her life, while John Buchan's friends, who had unbounded faith in his future, looked coldly at the whisperers.

On the bright mid-July day in 1907, when we were married, we had known each other for several years. I have described elsewhere[1] our first meetings, which went a little awkwardly, and our subsequent friendship, and our engagement which lasted a year.

We were always happy when we were together, but John had difficulties with his mother, who was deeply hurt that my father-in-law, who was a Presbyterian Minister, was not permitted to take any share in our marriage service. I am glad to say that when our eldest son was married in 1948 at St. Margaret's, Westminster, a Presbyterian Minister did take part in the service, a hopeful sign of greater unity among the churches.

The fact that I was a member of the Church of England was hard for my mother-in-law to swallow, and she was not a woman who resigned herself to any kind of checkmate in life without endless sighs and a good deal of argument, so that John had had in some ways an uneasy time at home. He spent part of the year of our engagement in lodgings in Edinburgh, going daily to Nelson's printing and publishing works at Parkside in order to learn the business with his usual thoroughness. He was devoted to Tommy Nelson, who had a variety of talents as well as great personal charm. He was a bold rider to hounds, an admirable fisherman and a shrewd and keen business man. He had also a profound interest in the lives of the men and women who worked at Parkside. Tommy Nelson's death in the first World War was an event which caused deep sadness to all those who had ever come in contact with him. But we were some years away from this and Parkside was, for John, always a happy and interesting place to work in.

In London John lived in Temple Gardens until our marriage.

[1] See *John Buchan: by His Wife and Friends.*

His rooms, which he shared with Harold Baker and Austin Smyth, an austere and charming Greek scholar who was Librarian to the House of Commons, gave an impression of cosy bachelor comfort, with dark walls and carpets and deep leather chairs. In order to get to them it was necessary to climb endless dark and dirty staircases; but the changing view of the river from their windows was always enchanting.

I went to many tea-time parties there before and after our engagement. These tea parties had their slightly alarming side, as the three youthful hosts had exacting conversational standards, and were down on any silliness or shallowness of mind. A naïve remark might always be repeated to a wider circle of clever and mocking people. However, I survived conversationally, somehow.

My mother (I cannot now quite imagine why) thought it would be fitting if I drove to and from the church in the Grosvenor family coach. The Westminsters kindly acceded to her request, and in this splendid and old-fashioned vehicle she and I made our way to St. George's, Hanover Square, gazed at with respectful awe by the passers by.

We were married by Cosmo Lang, then Bishop of Stepney, and John insisted upon having the thirteenth chapter of Corinthians read. He refused to allow the Bishop to give an address. "You never know," he remarked, "what a Bishop will say."

After the ceremony we stood for a moment in the sunlit porch of the great church before climbing into the coach. We had no idea where our steps would lead us. The future veiled its face. We could not know that after many years of complete happiness together John would lie in state in the capital of another country, while our youngest son and three other Canadian officers stood on guard round the coffin.

INDEX

Date Due

Printed in the USA
CPSIA information can be obtained
at www.ICGtesting.com
LVHW022339170124
769041LV00015B/1075